A History of Britain in 100 Dogs

To Saxon, and all the other dogs

First published 2016

The History Press
The Mill, Brimscombe Port
Stroud, Gloucestershire, GL5 2QG
www.thehistorypress.co.uk

British Library Cataloguing in Publication Data.
A catalogue record for this book is available from the British
Library.

ISBN 978 0 7509 6489 0

Cover design Jemma Cox
Layout design Katie Beard
Printed in China

A HISTORY OF BRITAIN IN 100 DOGS

EMMA WHITE

The History Press

Acknowledgements

There are so many people who deserve thanks for their efforts to provide help and information for this book. My interest in dogs as a historical subject goes back a few years to my MA dissertation on dogs during the Great War. Thanks are therefore due to Robert Brunsdon for planting the initial thought and continuing to support it.

Many libraries, museum, archives and charities around the country have helped me, supplying information and illustrations. On my many visits, especially at North Tuddenham, I was greeted with great kindness and interest in my project, and my gratitude to them in assisting me is unlimited.

Many of my friends and fellow researchers from the University of Birmingham, lovingly known as 'The Old BUMS' (The Old Birmingham University Masters Students), as well as my PhD supervisor Dr Ross Wilson at the University of Chichester, have played their part in finding, reading and of course listening at various points along this journey.

Thanks is also due to Dr Bryan Cummins who has always been very supportive and willing to share his immense knowledge and research on dogs. His help in proofreading this book was invaluable.

My friends and colleagues in the West Sussex County Council Library Service have searched for articles and most importantly humoured all of my 'doggie' stories told throughout the office! You have all been so kind and patient with me – thank you.

Thanks to the team at The History Press, especially Sophie Bradshaw, for asking me to write this book; without them, I would not be in this position.

My final thanks, and probably the most important, is to my family who have always been very supportive of my continuing endeavours to learn new things. My parents, sister and my partner have been part of this journey and also share my affections for our wonderful dog Saxon, to whom this book is dedicated.

Introduction

I hope this book will be enjoyable to anyone interested in the way that dogs are a part of our lives and our history, whether the reader is curious about breeds or famous individual canines, but also to those with a more general interest.

Many of these chapters cover important periods in time as they relate to dogs, while others simply illustrate their part in momentous occasions. With so many stories to choose from, it was impossible to include them all and so I was forced to narrow them down to my personal favourites; any omission of certain accounts or breeds is purely due to space issues and not meant to cause any offense. The tales included range from those with documentary evidence to those of pure legend and everything in between: dogs with whom we have grown up on our TV screens, those we have read about or others we may have seen on the news. Some famous canines are found within these pages, along with those who are unnamed or whose real identity remains unknown.

This was never intended to be a breed companion, and as such many breeds that we know today will not be found here. There is a wealth of information available for anyone wanting to study the history of a breed, and there are some suggestions in the references at the end. The aim of this book is to show the long journey that we have shared with all kinds of dogs in Britain, and everything they have done and still do for us today.

It has been a pleasure to learn and research the stories of all the dogs here, brought together under the common umbrella of our history. Over the months, I have formed a new appreciation of the abilities and nature of dogs, which I hope to share with you. Some of the stories have made me laugh out loud while others have brought me to tears, sometimes of joy, but not always. I hope that you will laugh and cry with me as you read, but above all understand the amazing part that dogs play in our lives, no matter what century we live in.

Remember, around every corner, at every important juncture in our history, there will be a dog somewhere, and hopefully someday it will be included in a book like this.

Emma White

2016

1|Ancient Dogs

It is difficult to exactly ascertain the number of breeds that were in existence in ancient Britain. There are many different accounts from historians, many of them not contemporaries, and, of course, the breeds that were in Britain at this time would look very different from their modern-day counterparts.

It is believed that in the Celtic world many breeds existed, both large and small, suggesting that even then dogs could have been kept as pets as well as working animals.[1] Regardless of if this was true, the main purpose of dogs at this time was to aid man in his daily life and leisure pursuits.

Byzantine mosaic of a musician with his dog. (John Copland, Shutterstock) *Opposite:* A mosaic of a Roman dog on a lead. (Mary Evans Picture Library)

Hunting would have been a key component of daily life, especially for leading individuals, and large dogs would run alongside horses to aid in the pursuit of game. These dogs could flush out small prey, wear down the pursued or chase them into snares. This activity was not only for enjoyment but also provided food and animal skins for bedding and decoration, as well as keeping the number of potential pests down.

The Greek writer Strabo (c.64 BC–c.AD 21), in his colossal writings about the world that cover Britain and Gaul (now mainly modern-day France), mentions indigenous dogs. Part of his description of Britain is worth reproducing here:

The greatest portion of this island is level and woody, although many tracts are hilly. It produces corn, cattle, gold, silver, and iron, which things are brought thence, and also skins and slaves, and dogs sagacious in hunting; the Kelts [sic] use these, as well as their native dogs, for the purposes of war.[2]

Strabo's words clearly indicate the presence of native dogs for war, those which were possibly taken back to Rome by Caesar as fighting dogs. These could have been ancestors of the mastiff or the bulldog, two of the oldest British breeds.

2 | Mastiffs

Mastiffs were dogs of war and accompanied the Celts who fought against Caesar when he landed in Britain in 55 and 54 BC. The respect for the mastiff is shown by the Romans taking the breed from Britain back to Rome to fight in their arenas.

Above: A large English mastiff. (Susan Schmitz, Shutterstock)
Right: Charles V of Spain, who received over 400 Mastiffs to help fight the French. (Library of Congress, LC-USZ62-113618)
Below: Victorian wood engraving of a mastiff. (Wellcome Library, London)

The breed of the Roman era would not resemble the one we have today and therefore many modern accounts speak of a 'mastiff-type dog'. However, the dog was certainly large and strong, as it was said to be able to break the neck of a bull.

The mastiff breed is discussed in *The Master of Game*, a book written by nobleman Edward of Norwich, 2nd Duke of York, between 1406 and 1413, which deals with the care, training and employment of hounds for hunting (medieval pets and hunting will be further discussed in another chapter). Edward consigned the mastiff breed to protection of the household, as he felt their nose to be inadequate for proper hunting, and so the breed was covered in only one page.[3]

Mastiffs have historically been valued by royalty. Charles V of Spain was said to have received 400 mastiffs in iron collars from Henry VIII to help fight him against the French during the Siege of Valencia.

The bull mastiff we know today derives from the original mastiffs. It is possible that mastiffs and the English bulldog have a joint ancestry.

Mastiff.

3 | Bayeux Tapestry

The Bayeux Tapestry is an iconic artefact recounting the lead up to the Norman Conquest and the Battle of Hastings in 1066. It is synonymous with a period of British history when noblemen fought for the throne of England and the country laid claim to parts of France that would be bitterly contested for the next 400 years, ending with the Hundred Years War.

The Bayeux Tapestry tells the story of William the Conqueror's succession to the English throne and illustrates his divine right to the throne as named successor of Edward the Confessor. The tapestry is 229ft long, 19in tall and weighs 772lb.[4] It covers the period from 1064 to 1066 and is thought to be incomplete, with the final scene, possibly showing William's coronation on Christmas Day 1066, having been lost over the centuries.

Although known as a tapestry, it is more correctly an embroidery and is now thought to have been produced either entirely or at least partly by English needlewomen. Historians have tried for many years to trace its existence, but the first 400 years of the tapestry's life remain shrouded in mystery and uncertainty,

Bayeux Tapestry detail showing the dogs in the border. (Myrabella)

although it is widely thought to have been produced under the orders of Odo of Bayeux, half-brother of William and later Earl of Kent. The first documentary evidence of its existence is in an inventory of the treasures of Bayeux Cathedral in around 1476, where the tapestry is listed as item 262. A translation of the entry tells us the following:

> Item, a very long and narrow textile that is embroidered with images and inscriptions that show the conquest of England, which is hung around the nave of the church the day and octave of the Feast of Relics.[5]

The movements of the tapestry over the centuries have been numerous, and during conflict and revolution it has often been taken for safekeeping and put back on display as a sign of victory or peace. Napoleon is said to have had the tapestry moved to Paris so he could use it as inspiration for planning an invasion of Britain.

Along with many other parts of daily life, such as eating, hunting and agriculture, dogs are portrayed as part of the story of the Norman Conquest. These are most likely to be hounds for hunting, a key part of a nobleman's life, and seem to

resemble a greyhound-type breed. The dogs appear both in the main scenes and in the top and bottom borders of the tapestry. Near the beginning of the work, when Harold is heading for the coast, his pack of hounds is shown leading the way. Similarly, when Harold is shown eating his final meal on land before leaving for France, two dogs are shown being carried on to the ship.

The number of dogs counted in the tapestry can vary from totals in the thirties to the fifties. A number at the lower end is probably more accurate, as some of the dogs are difficult to distinguish from other animals. Livestock as well as mythical creatures are dotted around the borders of the work, and many can possibly be mistaken for dogs.

The inclusion of dogs in this important historical artefact, which in its time was a demonstration of the right of William to the throne of England, shows the significance of these hounds in daily life. In a tapestry like this, where the needleworkers would have likely had dictated to them the scenes and themes to be included (such as divine right and victory in battle), the value of dogs is clear. That they represent wealth and importance is clearly evident from their inclusion on the ships coming across the Channel.

4 | Domesday Book

Domesday Book derived its name from the Day of Judgement. As the book had all of the details about who owned what and where, it was a document from which there could be no appeal regarding its judgement. Nowadays it forms the basis of our national land ownership. At over 900 years old it is still admissible as evidence in legal proceedings relating to land entitlement.[6]

Page from Domesday Book for Warwickshire,

The Domesday survey was commissioned by William the Conqueror (1066–87) in around 1086 for the purpose of assessing the lands that belonged to the king and his people. The survey was conducted in minute detail, with commissioners visiting all areas of the country to establish who owned what and how much it was worth.

However, the detail of the survey did not stop there. A surviving version of the regional returns for Ely Abbey contains a copy of the commissioner's brief, showing what he was instructed to find out:

The name of the place, who held it before 1066, and now.
How many hides. (Land unit around 120 acres.) How many ploughs.
How many villagers, cottagers and slaves, how many free men and Freemen.
How much woodland, meadow and pasture. How many mills and fishponds.
How much has been added or taken away. What the total value was and is.
How much each free man or Freeman had or has.
All threefold, before 1066, when King William gave it, and now.[7]

There are in fact two Domesday Books: Little and Great. Little Domesday covered Essex, Suffolk and Norfolk and is much more detailed than its larger counterpart. Great Domesday covers a much larger area of the country. However, it is not complete, as large cities such as London, Winchester and Bristol are not recorded.[8] Other areas, such as Cumberland and Westmoreland, which were not yet part of England, were never surveyed.[9]

In the returns for Gloucestershire and Warwickshire, evidence can be found for the existence of dogs in everyday life. In the return for Cheltenham, details include the number of villagers, mills, ploughs and slaves. The entry ends with the revenue payable by the area: before 1066 it paid £9 5s and 3,000 loaves for its dogs; then it pays £20, twenty cows, twenty pigs and 16s for bread.[10] Under King Edward the custom fee for dogs in Cheltenham was paid in kind, in the form of cakes of dog-bread, but under King William this had been commuted to a monetary fee of 16s. Throughout the Domesday survey there seems to have been a move from the payments received in kind, such as bread or animals, in Edward the Confessor's time to monetary payments in William the Conqueror's reign.

Cheltenham was not the only place where the customs due for dogs are mentioned; in Warwick, for example, '23 pounds' were paid for the custom of dogs. Therefore dogs have raised funds for government since at least 1086 until the modern dog licence was finally abolished in the 1980s, over 900 years later.

An early depiction of a dog, c. 1100.

Writing Domesday Book, from a nineteenth-century illustration.

5 | The Laws of the Forest

From before Norman times, laws have been in place to protect and restrict the use of designated forests throughout Britain. All forest belonged to the king and, as such, the right to hunt in them was held by the monarch alone. He could bestow rights, however, to nobles for hunting a certain amount of wild beasts per year.

Below: The original seal from a copy of the Magna Carta, showing King John hunting. (British Library, Add. 4838) *Opposite:* Early Georgian print of dogs hunting in the forest; one has caught a deer. (Wellcome Library, London)

In the time of King Cnut (1016–35) laws were put down to protect forest land. However, it was William the Conqueror (1066–87) and his heirs who more strictly enforced them and extended the area of the country which they covered.

By Henry II's reign (1154–89) over a quarter of the whole of England was considered part of royal forest land – and therefore land of the king.[11] It was not necessarily forested as we would understand the term today, and could be fields and pasture. Declaring these areas as royal forest land stopped ordinary people from using the space to graze animals and collect firewood for cooking. Before this time, those who owned the land had been free to hunt on it as they wished.

There were, of course, consequences for all those who lived on and near this protected land. Many of those who disregarded the laws and were caught were punished and hefty fines were levied (see the chapter on financial rolls for more on this). Punishments could be more severe than fines, however, and the price for taking deer was the death penalty. Moreover, for those who lived on royal forest land, their ability to own a dog was compromised. Of course, at this time, most dogs were kept for security, working or hunting reasons.

It was accepted in all of the forest laws that dogs were an important asset and it seems there was no restriction on who could actually own one, just that it could only be near the dwelling for security of property and not used to hunt. However, this meant that harsh penalties and even mutilation of the dogs could be imposed for those living within the confines of the royal forest land to ensure it could not be used in a way that went against the laws. Mastiffs are specifically mentioned;

Early German woodcut of a man and his dog hunting in the forest. (Wellcome Library, London)

this is the breed that seemed to cause most concern in the forest and also that was most common at the time.[12]

Under the forest laws the owners of mastiff dogs were forced to have their dog mutilated in order to stop them from hunting. This mutilation was termed 'expeditating'. The manner of expeditating dogs is mentioned in Carta de Foresta, Artic. 6:

Three Claws of the Fore-feet shall be cut off by the Skin: And accordingly the same is now used, but setting one of his Fore-feet upon a piece of Wood eight Inches thick, and a Foot square, and then setting a Chizel of two Inches broad upon the three Claws of his Fore-foot, to strike them off at one Blow; and this is the manner of expeditating Mastiffs.[13]

In the time of Cnut, a different practice was used to lame such dogs, which was to cut the hamstring.[14] 'Little dogs' are also mentioned as being allowed in the forest in Cnut's time, but there is no further description of what breed these dogs were.

The Magna Carta of 1215 is well known to most people, if only by name. From the reign of King John (1199–1216), its contents created more rights for the barons, who were attempting to restore rights they felt had been stripped from their families after the invasion of William the Conqueror. The charter only became known as Magna Carta in 1217, in order to distinguish itself from a smaller piece of legislation that had been removed from it, which was called the Carta de Foresta (or Charter of the Forest).

The Charter of the Forest was signed in 1217 by the child king Henry III (born 1207, ruled 1216–72) and gave back the right to use the forest. The rights contained within the charter were important for a wider section of society than just the barons and noblemen. It actually gave rights to freemen to use the forests for fuel, grazing and pasture, and protected them from the higher classes. The death penalty for stealing deer was also removed. Relating to dogs, the charter softened the approach to expediation, stating that this was only necessary in those areas of forest where it had been carried out since the reign of Henry II. This meant that those areas that were no longer forest under the terms of the charter, which was most of the area Henry II had expanded it to encompass, no longer needed to expeditate their mastiffs.[15] It did not, however, reverse the need to expeditate mastiffs residing in the areas still classed at royal forests. During this period, the punishment for not having a dog expeditated was no more than 3s. However, in today's money, this would roughly equate to over £80.[16]

English mastiff with a forest in the background. The claws of these dogs were struck off to prevent them from hunting in the king's forests. (Wellcome Library, London)

A further set of laws, The Assises and Customs of the Forest (c.1278), repealed some of the rules relating to dogs. Mastiffs and greyhounds could now be kept within the forest unexpeditated, as long as they had a lawful claim to do so by grant of the king.[17]

The main source for the forest laws is John Manwood's *Treatise of the Forest Laws*. Written in 1598, Manwood's aim was to put together all of the laws, both past and present, that governed the forest into one book. The book went through several reprints and was again edited and the language modernised for a 1717 edition. His work has been used here to describe some of the laws pertaining to the keeping of dogs within the royal forests.

By Tudor times, most of the laws relating to the forest had been repealed and those remaining mainly served to protect timber. However, some clauses on the 1217 charter were still in force in the 1970s, making it the longest statue in English law.

6 | The Legend of Gelert

The message at the heart of the Legend of Gelert is one that has been repurposed many times over the centuries. It is a tale of regret and the consequences of actions carried out in the heat of the moment without knowing the full circumstances.

Below: An engraving of Gelert, the dog of Prince Llewelyn. (Mary Evans Picture Library)

Historians debate whether the story is true or just a vehicle for the meaning it carries, but one thing is for certain: if you go to Beddgelert, at the foot of Snowdonia, you can see the memorial to Gelert, which is at his supposed final resting place.

Putting aside whether or not the legend is true, what it portrays are the characteristics that any owner would admire in their dog: friendship, protection and loyalty.

What breed of dog Gelert was is not definitively known. However, his bravery and size in the legend implies that he was a wolf/dog cross. The legend says that Llewelyn the Great had a beautiful dog named Gelert who had been a gift from King John in 1205. The dog always accompanied Llewelyn when he went hunting, and one day his absence was sorely noticed. When the prince returned home he was angry at the dog, who met him at the door of Llewelyn's infant child's room, stained in blood. Llewelyn called out to his son but received no reply. Upon seeing the room in disarray, he thrust his sword into Gelert in anguish for perpetrating this foul deed. The dog died instantly and as the prince rushed into the room he heard his son cry. He searched for the boy and finally found him covered by a blanket, with the body of a dead wolf nearby. He knew instantly that

Above: A postcard showing the story of Gelert. (Mary Evans Picture Library). *Below:* Gelert's grave. (The History Press)

Gelert had protected his son from this ravenous wolf and that in killing his dog he had betrayed the friendship and loyalty between them. As penance, Llewelyn built a chapel and raised a tomb to Gelert; the spot where this chapel is thought to have been is called Beddgelert or 'the grave of Gelert'.

7 | Financial Records

As is the way with most countries, the majority of the best-preserved records are those that relate to finance and the income and expenditure of a government. This has been the same for hundreds, if not thousands, of years and today some of the records that shed the most light on the lives of those before us are those which relate to money. Domesday Book was just one example of this.

The Fine Rolls of King Henry III (reigned 1216–72) are a fantastic source of information for the governance of the kingdom in this period. The earliest was created in 1199 and there is an almost continual sequence from then onwards. These rolls, rather than just containing fines levied for crimes, show the way in which life was changing in Britain, with permission being granted by the king for marriages, inheritance of land and titles and the setting up of markets, as well as ownership of land and rights. These privileges were often gained by a monetary payment, and these rolls are the evidence of those payments. The Fine Rolls have been transcribed and made publicly available by a project between The National Archives, Canterbury Christ Church University and Kings College, London. This wonderful resource allows an insight into the medieval world in a digital age.[18]

Two examples from this period exemplify not only the role of dogs in society, but also the problems that could occur if you did not have the correct authority. Hunting, as already discussed, was a favoured pastime by all classes. However, during and after William the Conqueror's rule the right to hunt, especially on land or designated forest owned by the king, was very difficult to obtain.

The first instance, from the seventh year of Henry III's reign, describes one Hugh de Gournay, whose entire land and property was to be placed in the hands of the king for safekeeping until further orders from Henry III. Hugh de Gournay had hunted in the Chase of Bristol with hounds, which was against the forest law as he had no permission from the king.[19]

A further example nearly ten years later shows the continuing problem of unlawful hunting. Roger of Dauntsey was ordered to pay 60 marks (which equated to 800s or £40 and would be over £20,000 today). Roger's crime was to have been caught trespassing in the king's forest of Windsor with his greyhounds, hunting the king's venison. This huge fine was extracted from Roger at 100s (£5) for the first two years, followed by £10 a year until the balance was paid off.[20]

The fines were huge amounts of money. However, Hugh and Roger were not peasants and both owned large estates. It is likely that both Hugh and Roger's families had accompanied the conqueror to England and so their titles and land ownership stemmed from this period, as did many of the families of wealthy land-owners during this period.

Early engraving showing a hunting greyhound biting a fox, who in turn is biting a bird. (Wellcome Library, London)

8 | Medieval Hunting

Issues surrounding medieval hunting, such as the Laws of the Forest, are discussed in other chapters, but it is worth exploring the wider role of hunting as both a status symbol and a medieval leisure pursuit.

The upper classes kept horses and hounds specifically for hunting. Although an important show of status and wealth, hunting actually prepared many noble young men for war.[21]

Edward of Norwich, 2nd Duke of York, was passionate about hunting and believed there was a right way for the hunter to conduct himself as well as his hounds. His earlier mentioned *The Master of Game* set out the right way to hunt and care for hounds, as well as their nature and discussion of the quarry they should pursue. It is the earliest English book specifically on hunting. Although a vast part of his book was a translation of the work of Gaston III, Count of Foix's *Le Livre de Chasse*, Edward added his own experiences and some interesting reasoning about the merits of hunting. These are very important in defining the role of hunting during this period of history.[22]

Edward believed that by following rules and partaking in the good sport of hunting, man could avoid succumbing to the seven deadly sins, a theory which he discusses in the prologue. Idleness was thought to be one way that men turned to evil thoughts and deed, but, Edward advised, through the preparation and act of hunting there was no time to be idle or have wandering thoughts of anything other than the task in hand.[23]

He also proclaimed that men who took part in hunting were much happier in their lives, because, 'the hunter riseth in the morning, and he sees as sweet and fair morn and clear weather and bright'.[24] He goes even further, saying that 'hunters go to Paradise when they die, and live in this world more joyfully than any other men'.[25] Edward died at the Battle of Agincourt fighting with Henry V, whom he reportedly saved in forfeit of his own life.

A medieval miniature showing King John hunting with hounds. (British Library, Cotton Claudius D. II)

9 | Religious Houses

In the medieval period, pets were just as cherished as today, and even those who had taken religious orders sought the companionship of animals in their lives. Many nunneries were not only populated by those who had chosen a religious life from a young age, but also by those who had led worldly lives before turning to religion. Therefore they had experience of pets and other customs which would have been difficult to give up.

Dogs were the favourite pet amongst the religious houses; there were several injunctions against nuns bringing puppies into services. (British Library, 003599001)

Whatever the specific reasons for pets being in the nunneries, those in charge (namely the bishops) struggled, unsuccessfully, against the keeping of pets. In a society where it was common for ladies to attend church with a lapdog and for men to have a hawk on their wrist, it is hardly surprising that nuns had their own pets at the nunnery.

Dogs were the favourite animals among the religious houses.[26] At Keldholme and Rosedale in Yorkshire, the two priories of Cistercians nuns were reprimanded against the keeping of pets, especially puppies, by their respective archbishops in the fourteenth century.[27] Keldholme experienced a number of rebellious nuns in the early part of the century. In one visitation report of 1301, the archbishop had found four nuns to be 'incorrigible rebels' and these nuns were scattered to other houses to perform the penances ordered of them.[28] The rest of the decade remained quiet at Keldholme and, after a visitation in 1314, the nuns were reminded not to wear secular finery or anything except that which was fit for their religious purpose. The prioress was also instructed that 'puppies were excluded from entering quire, cloister, and other places, and nuns who offended in regard to this were to be punished'.[29] In 1315 the prioress and sub-prioress of Rosedale Priory were similarly ordered not to allow puppies into areas of the church that would 'impede the service and hinder the devotion of the nuns'.[30]

10 | The Canterbury Tales

The Canterbury Tales were written by Geoffrey Chaucer (*c.* 1340–1400). This work was very popular at the time as it was written in Middle English, the language that everyday people would have spoken, rather than the French and Latin that were spoken at the king's court and usually used as the written language. Chaucer went abroad in 1359 and was taken prisoner during a battle of the Hundred Years War with France.

The Canterbury Tales is a famous long poem in which many different people from medieval life are encountered, all of whom are on a pilgrimage to the shrine of Thomas Beckett in Canterbury Cathedral. The individuals at the start of *The Canterbury Tales* are in The Tabard in Southwark, from where they travel together with the host of the inn and Chaucer. It is thought that Chaucer wanted to include more stories than he actually finished; from the description in the prologue, each pilgrim was to tell two tales on the way to Canterbury and two on the way back. Around thirty individuals are described in the prologue, making this a monumental project. Additionally, the individual tales differ in their style depending on who is telling them. The stories cover a wide range of themes from all over Europe and further afield, contemporary stories which Chaucer himself would have read.[31]

The individual tales, although interesting and amusing, are not where we can find our connection to dogs. Chaucer used a prologue at the beginning of his work to introduce the characters and it is here that we can see how dogs were viewed in medieval life and their place within it. The first reference is in his description of the Prioress. Chaucer begins:

Sixteenth-century portrait of Chaucer. (British Library, Add. 5141)

There also was a Nun, a Prioress,
Her way of smiling very simple and coy …

1402

He discusses the way in which she spoke and ate before continuing:

> She used to weep if she but saw a mouse
> Caught in a trap, if it were dead or bleeding.
> And she had little dogs she would be feeding
> With roasted flesh, or milk, or fine white bread.
> Sorely she wept if one of them were dead
> Or someone took a stick and made it smart;[32]

Chaucer depicts the image of a nun who had an interest in worldly things and wore fine clothes, against the ideals of who a nun should be. The way in which she treated her lapdogs, with fine food and tender affections, was certainly not befitting a nun.

Soon after the Prioress, Chaucer describes the Monk in the party, saying:

> A Monk there was, one of the finest sort
> Who rode the country; hunting as his sport ...
> This Monk was therefore a good man to horse;
> Greyhounds he had, as swift as birds, to course.
> Hunting a hare or riding at a fence
> Was all his fun he spared for no expense.[33]

Detail from the *Canterbury Tales* mural at the Library of Congress, showing prioress with dogs. (Library of Congress, LC-DIG-highsm-03190)

Although the descriptions of dogs in these examples are in relation to the negative aspects of their owners, who should have not enjoyed such extravagances due to their religious vocations, what they do tell us is that dogs were in use as pets and for hunting in this period. Moreover, it teaches us that even if we think we know what the role of someone in society is, especially when thinking historically, in reality this may not have always been the case!

Chaucer died on 25 October 1400 and was buried in Westminster Abbey. An elaborate monument was erected in the following century. This interment was the first in an area of the abbey that has become known as Poets' Corner.

Chaucer's tomb in Westminster Abbey.

11 | The War Dog of the Battle of Agincourt

One prestigious line of mastiffs, known as the Lyme Hall mastiffs, can trace their origins to a legendary dog that supposedly bravely protected his wounded master at the Battle of Agincourt in 1415.

The faithful companion guarded the wounded Sir Piers de Legh from the fierce French men at arms until his servants and comrades could get to him. Sir Piers died in 1422 in Paris and the dog was returned home to Lyme Hall, in Cheshire (now owned by The National Trust) where he sired the first of the now famous Lyme Hall mastiffs. The connection with the breed is even preserved in glass, with a stained-glass window bearing the image of the mastiff at Lyme Hall.

Lyme Hall, Cheshire.
(Snowshill, Shutterstock)

This great tale is, unfortunately, probably just that, a tale told to further the reputation of the de Legh lineage during the turmoil the monarchy found itself in during the centuries after the battle. There is no historical evidence to prove the existence of this dog on the battlefield. However, many dog owners would attest to the characteristics shown by the dog in the legend as being true qualities of a loyal canine companion.

The de Leghs owned Lyme Hall for 550 years, and magnificent paintings of some of the mastiffs of the Lyme Hall line adorn the walls. The strain became extinct after the First World War.[34]

Victorian print after 'Morning at Agincourt' by Sir John Gilbert.

12 | Dogs in Heraldry

For centuries, coats of arms have been used as grand illustrations of family achievements, wealth and importance. It was during the reign of William the Conqueror that the use of heraldry started to evolve, and therefore much of the language describing it has its roots in Norman French.

The original purpose for coats of arms was not so grand or prestigious. Instead, they were designed as a quick way to identify knights and leaders through the smoke and ferocity of the battlefield. Simple geometric patterns which were easily identifiable were the most common at this time; they became more elaborate as heraldry evolved.

Coats of arms are often extremely detailed and it takes a great deal of expertise to decipher their meanings. They contain all manner of different animals, from mythical monsters and exotic creatures to more recognisable domestic beasts. Just as interesting as the type of animal chosen is their placement within the design, which can also have an effect on the meaning. Even the display of the teeth or claw of the creature helps to distinguish between different families and give further depth to the coat of arms.

The Carter crest depicting a Talbot dog.

In English heraldry, the talbot was a favourite breed to be illustrated on heraldic crests.[35] This breed was a medieval hunting dog that is now extinct.

Coats of Arms and the use of a certain heraldic crest are granted to a specific person and therefore the right to use it continues down the ancestral line. These grants are only given by the College of Arms (founded in 1484) and it is an expensive process to obtain the documentation necessary to obtain one. However, nowadays, many people design their own crests. Although these are not official, they are extremely popular given the recent rise of genealogy.

In 1789 Mr William Phillips, a wealthy businessman of Cavendish Square, London, used the image of a Newfoundland on his crest after his life was saved by such a dog. He was bathing in the sea at Portsmouth when he was seized by cramp and unable to swim. The man who was attending the bathing machine (today's equivalent of a lifeguard) jumped in to help but, although he made contact, he was unable to help Phillips and was only just able to save himself.[36] Two men with a boat were watching the scene and, while bystanders urged them to help, they refused to unless they were paid.[37] Meanwhile, a Newfoundland dog that happened to be on the seashore saw Phillips in difficulty and jumped in. After swimming to him, the dog took hold of Phillips' bathing cap in his teeth and pulled

The canine coat of arms above the entrance to King's College, Cambride. (Graham Taylor)

him safely back to shore.[38] A grateful Phillips purchased the dog from his owner and the two became firm friends.

Phillips used the image of the dog on his coat of arms, along with the motto *Virum Extuli Mari*, which means 'I have rescued a man from the sea'. He engraved his cutlery and even embroidered his tablecloths in recognition of the canine who had saved him. Phillips also commissioned a painting showing the dog, whom he named 'Friend'.

The Newfoundland breed, native to Newfoundland (which is now part of Canada). With its webbed feet the Newfoundland breed is an excellent swimmer and, although early English types would have been smaller in size than today's examples, was capable of being a working-dog breed.

Newspapers across the country reported on the rescue of William Phillips, from Hereford to Derby and Chester to Dublin. Even the *Annual Register*, which detailed political and historical events and literature of the year, deemed it a fitting tale to enter into its 1789 volume.

A larger Newfoundland dog.
(Flikr Commons)

13 | Greyhounds

Sight hounds have been used for chasing game for hundreds of years and more recently for racing. Greyhounds and their ancestors are the most famous and recognisable of these breeds.

Much has been written about the greyhound and its nature. Edward, Duke of York was positive about the use of this breed in hunting and even described how to take care of them. He also wrote that the goodness of a greyhound comes from their courage and the nature bestowed on them by their parents.[39] He leaves a wonderful sentence at the end of his chapter on the nature of greyhounds: 'He shall be good and kindly *and clean*, glad and joyful and playful, well willing and goodly to all manner of folk save to the wild beasts to whom he should be fierce, spiteful and eager.'[40]

The Forest Laws of England, which were written by the Anglo-Norman rulers, prohibited ownership of these dogs, so that only a 'gentleman' could keep them. An old Welsh proverb also speaks of the reputation and prominence that owning a greyhound could bestow on a person: 'You may know a gentleman by his horse, his hawk, and his greyhound.'[41]

"Gray-Hound" in a 1658 English woodcut. (University of Houston Libraries)

It is probable that the reputation of the greyhound as a gentleman's dog comes from its use during hunting, which was certainly a nobleman's sport from the Anglo-Norman period onwards, if not before. However, another reason for the status of this breed could be from its religious connections, as the greyhound is the only breed identified in the Bible (Proverbs 30: 29–31). In the King James Bible 'Greyhound' is the translation given as one of the four stately beings (the others are a lion, a goat, and a king), although other versions translate this passage to be many different animals, such as a rooster or a horse. Considering the claim of the

A group of the smaller Italian Greyhound dogs. (Luigi Panico Photography)

greyhound, it clearly fits the description of a very stately animal and is also one that has been highly prized for centuries.

The History of Four-footed Beasts by Edwin Topsel (published in 1655) starts the section of dogs with the 'Gray-Hound' saying they 'deserveth the first place; for such are the conditions of this Dog ... he is reasonably sented to finde out, speedy and quick of foot to follow; and fierce and strong to take and overcome: and yet silent, coming upon his prey at unawares.'[42]

Dame Juliana Berners, who is reputedly the author of *The Book of St Albans* (1486), also shared her ideas on what character and nature a good greyhound should possess:

A grehound shold be heeded lyke a snake
And neckyd lyke a drake,
Footed lyke a catte,
Taylld lyke a ratte,
Syded lyke a teme,
And chynyd like a beme.[43]

Greyhound racing has been popular for decades and still is today, although the breed's original role in hunting has not been widespread for many decades, even before the law banning the use of dogs in the sport. Historically, there have been many prestigious hunting races for greyhounds, the most important being the Waterloo Cup, which began in 1836. This was an annual coursing event where sixty-four greyhounds from Britain and Ireland would compete. This competition continued up until the ban in 2005.

Greyhounds hunting. (Flikr Commons)

Anecdotes of greyhounds also abound in connection with past monarchs. According to legend, Richard II (1377–99) had a prized greyhound that would not show affection to anyone but the king. But, on the appearance of Henry, Duke of Lancaster the animal changed his allegiance immediately. Henry had gone to Flint Castle in Wales to accept Richard's surrender and the greyhound fawned over the stranger and eventually left with him. It was thought that the greyhound had foreknowledge of the events to come, a belief that was strengthened when Henry deposed Richard II to become Henry IV (1399–1413).[44]

The 'Best in Show' category at Crufts was initiated at the show of 1928 and the first winner was a greyhound called Primley Sceptre who was owned by Herbert Whitley. The name derives from the estate he lived in: Primley, in Paignton, Devon. An animal lover and conservationist, Herbert Whitley began a conservation and educational park at his home, which is now Paignton Zoo.

14 | Turnspit Dogs

Centuries ago, dogs were used not only for their natural abilities for tasks such as tracking, herding and hunting, but for the propulsion power they could give to various wheel-driven machines.

To save a human from turning a roasting spit for hours in order to cook the meat, a contraption was designed that would allow a dog in a running wheel to turn the spit instead. At one time the role of this dog was so important that a turnspit dog was considered a separate and vital breed, and was a common part of the kitchen in both public houses and homes, as demonstrated in the work of John Caius, an English physician (1510–73). This is one of the earliest, if not *the* earliest, published works on English dogs, and in it he describes the breed's excellent service in the kitchen turning the spit, stating that they carry out their work so diligently that 'no drudge nor skullion can doe the feate more cunningly'.[45]

A description of the breed, which is now extinct, is contained in a work published in 1800. The dog:

… is generally long bodied, has short crooked legs, its tail curled upon its back, and is frequently spotted with black upon a blue-gray ground. It is peculiar in the colour of its eyes; the same Dog often having the iris of one eye black, and the other white.[46]

This description later notes that the use of the dog in kitchens was in decline, its role having been superseded by mechanisation.

A turnspit dog working.
(Henry Wigstead)

The work of these dogs was not easy, with one commentator suggesting that it could take three hours of constant turning for a large solid piece of beef to cook properly. Where these dogs were used daily to cook meat, they were often kept in pairs in order to alternate them each day. It is said that each dog knew its day to work, anyone would be hard-pressed to make a dog work on the wrong day and that this breed have been known to hunt out an absent worker whose 'shift' they had to cover in order to avenge their lost day off.[47] This is also thought to be the origin of the saying 'every dog has its day'.

Few examples of the dog-driven spit actually exist, and those that do are often found in public houses like the one at the George Inn in Lacock. Due to development in kitchen machinery, the breed was no longer required for the arduous job of turning the spit and therefore fell into decline and finally extinction. It was rare to find a dog performing this job by the 1860s, and they had all but vanished by 1900.

It is hard to know exactly what the breed looked like, but in Abergavenny Museum, the stuffed turnspit dog named Whiskey is thought to be the last remaining specimen. Although Whiskey differs from the description given in 1800, like with all dogs, a certain amount of change in a breed is expected over time.

The turnspit dog dressed as a chef proudly holds up a dish he has prepared. (Mary Evans Picture Library)

15 | Retrievers and Labradors

Retrievers are part of the group known as 'gun dogs'. Even though many are today used for a wide range of purposes, their original role was to retrieve game in the field after shooting. Many of the breeds which were devised for this purpose make excellent swimmers, as they would retrieve ducks and other water fowl that had been killed or wounded. They are generally wonderfully versatile dogs and carry out work today which wouldn't even have been imagined 100 years ago.

Golden retriever puppy. (Mikkel Bigandt, Shutterstock)

One of the best-known breeds falls into both categories: a Labrador retriever. This breed is consistently ranked as one of the most popular, both as a pet and a working dog, due to its versatility. A Labrador is a fantastic all-round dog, turning its paw to anything asked of it. Today their roles include use as a police dog for detecting drugs; as military dogs detecting explosives; and, perhaps the most recognisable, as a guide dog. Their role in aiding the blind has shown how capable this breed can be, and how, with training, they can achieve nearly any task asked of them. Guide dogs are not always Labradors, but it is the breed used in most publicity showing the world the capabilities of dogs and how they can be trained to help a wider range of people. Due to their popularity and, it has to be said, undeniable cuteness (especially as a puppy), Labrador retrievers have been used in many advertising roles, including toilet paper.

The Labrador enjoys the water and was thought to have originated from Newfoundland, where fishermen used a dog resembling it to retrieve fish. Despite its many skills as a working dog, it is also a popular choice as a pet because of its kind and gentle nature and love of children.

The golden retriever is also a hugely popular dog around the world. Like Labrador retrievers, they were originally used for retrieving game after shooting, but the versatility of this breed has made it an obvious choice for many roles, including as assistance dogs, military dogs, and as trackers. It wasn't until the early twentieth century, however, that the breed became known by its present name, having previously been known as 'yellow' retrievers and even shown as flat-coated retrievers in the show ring.

The flat-coated retriever is a fun-loving dog that isn't afraid of hard work. It was commonly associated with large estates as a gamekeeper's dog in the late nineteenth century. This is a very friendly dog that loves company, swimming and lots of exercise.

Georgian gun dogs in action.
(Wellcome Library, London)

Finally, meet the curly coated retriever. With its tight curls it is easily distinguishable from the rest of the group. These curls cover all of his body except his face, this coat making him virtually waterproof. It is thought that curly coated retrievers have been around for over 200 years and come from the crossing of various types of water spaniel and retrievers.[48]

Left: Hunting retriever. (Kirk Geisler, Shutterstock)

Below left: Labrador Retriever puppies in various colours. (ARTSILNSE, Shutterstock)

Below: Curly-coated retriever. (otsphoto, Shutterstock)

16 | The Tudors

Henry VIII was 18 when he became king in 1509. His elder brother Arthur had died in 1502, leaving him as heir to the throne. Despite only having five reigning monarchs, the Tudors held the throne – somewhat tumultuously – for over 100 years. As a family, the Tudors had great affection for animals and specifically dogs.

In 1526 the Eltham Ordinances were produced, named after the Eltham Palace where Cardinal Thomas Wolsey devised this plan to reform the court of Henry VIII. Among the ordinances, references about bringing dogs to court can be found: all dogs were to be banned except the lapdogs of ladies.[49] This type of toy dog may be related to the King Charles spaniel, which became a favourite of Charles II. If permission was obtained from the king to bring other dogs to court they had to be left in the kennels, so that the court could remain a pleasant place to be.[50]

Henry VIII's own pet dogs seem to have been rather mischievous, as they were often going missing. Two of his dogs, identified in accounts and papers relating to his reign, were guilty of this more than once. One dog, which was described as a spaniel, named Cut (sometimes spelt Cutte), went missing in 1530, and one of Queen Catherine of Aragon's servants was given 10s for returning the pet.[51]

Only three days later, another of the king's dogs (named Ball) was returned after he was lost in Waltham Forest and a payment of 5s was made to the person who returned him.[52] Cut again went astray in February the following year and a 'poor woman' was gifted 4s 8d for bringing him back.[53] In total these rewards would equate to over £300 in today's money.[54]

When Henry died in 1547, an inventory was taken of all his belongings, which listed a total of sixty-five dog leashes![55]

Anne Boleyn, Henry's second wife, is known to have enjoyed having pet dogs, the most notable of which was called Purquoy (or Purkoy). The dog had been a gift from Lady Lisle in 1534, as the queen had seen the dog while on a trip to France and had taken such a shine to it that she had requested it.[56] Although Lady Lisle was saddened to part with the dog, she hoped that in return the queen would

Eltham Palace, where the Eltham Ordinances were drafted. (Chris Jenner, Shutterstock)

Portrait of King Henry VIII. This volume was said to have been given by Anne Boleyn, when on the scaffold, to one of her maids of honour, a lady of the Wyat family. (British Library, Stowe 956, f.1v)

Opposite, top: Cardinal Wolsey. (Wellcome Library, London)

Opposite, bottom: Thomas Seymour. (Georgios Kollidas, Shutterstock)

favour her daughters by finding them positions in her household. This dog was reportedly a very rare breed in England at that time, and sadly met an unfortunate end by falling out of a window.

The penchant for dogs in the royal household continued with Henry's third wife, Jane Seymour, who died shortly after giving birth to the king's only male heir. The famous Whitehall mural, finished in 1537, showed a small white dog at her feet. The mural was painted by Hans Holbein the younger, but was destroyed when the Whitehall Palace was burnt down in 1698.[57] However, a copy of the mural had been made in the mid-seventeenth century by Remigius van Leemput, which is how we know what the original looked like. There is some controversy over the white dog at Jane's feet; it is debated whether it was added later when the mural was copied or was in fact part of the original painting.[58]

Another story from the Tudor era tells a much sadder tale. Edward VI, the young and sickly son of Henry VIII and Jane Seymour, who ascended the throne at the age of 9, was subject to an attempted kidnap attempt by his uncle. Edward's uncle, Thomas Seymour, claimed he had become concerned about the advice that his brother was giving their young nephew. However, it is more likely that Thomas wished to advance over his own brother, who currently had more control over Edward. Regardless of his reason, in an attempt to make the king see his point of view he staged a kidnap attempt in 1549. He was stopped by one of Edward's dogs, which attacked him as he was trying to enter the prince's bedroom and, in desperation, shot the dog.[59] Thomas Seymour was executed two months later on Tower Hill.[60]

17 | Hatch

The importance of dogs in society has been apparent for hundreds of years, and the Tudor period was no different. Even Henry VIII's prized warship the *Mary Rose* was home to a dog. However, the canine's existence was kept a secret for nearly 440 years while the ship lay at the bottom of the Solent. The magnificent ship saw thirty-four years' service before she sank in 1545[61] and had taken part in many skirmishes against both the French and Scottish navies.[62]

Life on board would have been very cramped, with a variety of people with different jobs all living together. In normal settings the ship would have had around 400 people on board but in times of war it could increase to up to 700.[63]

There are conflicting reports about how she came to sink in July 1545 during the Battle of the Solent, but what is sure is that hundreds of men lost their lives when she sank, with only around thirty-five surviving. Tudor divers attempted to salvage the ship, but all their attempts failed and she was left lying on her side on the seabed. Over time the exposed structure deteriorated leaving half the ship buried within fine silts that preserved her.

She was finally raised from the seabed in 1982, just 2km from the entrance to Portsmouth Harbour. During the underwater excavation, the skeleton of a dog was found outside the carpenter's cabin, in front of the sliding door. The dog would have been around 2 years old and was closely related to a terrier type of breed, similar to a Jack Russell.[64] The dog, after forensic examinations, has been proven to be male and not a female as originally thought.[65] He has been named 'Hatch' by archaeologists and is on display in the Mary Rose Museum within Portsmouth Historic Dockyard.

Hatch was the special guest of Crufts in 2010 and was on display for visitors to see before he returned to his permanent home within the Mary Rose Museum.

The skeleton of the
carpenter's dog, Hatch.
(The Mary Rose Trust)

During Henry VIII's reign, dogs would have been a familiar sight on board ships in order to keep the rat population down to stop the spread of disease. Hatch was a small dog and therefore perfect for this type of job. Although we would traditionally think of cats as vermin catchers, during this period cats were closely linked to witchcraft and had been outlawed by the Pope, therefore possession of one could be dangerous.

18 | Mary, Queen of Scots

When Elizabeth I ascended to the throne in 1559 on the death of her sister, she was to reign for forty-four years and ultimately bring the Tudor period to an end. She restored Protestantism as the religion of the nation and became head of the Church of England, as her father Henry VIII had been before her. For a significant portion of her reign, Elizabeth's cousin, Mary, Queen of Scots, had been a cause for concern and a figurehead of Catholic resistance to Elizabeth.

Mary was a widow and had spent most of her life in France, despite being heir to the Scottish throne. It was feared that if she married a figure in a strong Catholic nation she would have the power necessary to invade England and depose Elizabeth. However, Mary's choice in husbands proved unpopular: first to her cousin, Lord Darnley, who later died mysteriously (with Mary herself under suspicion) and then to Lord Bothwell, a man disliked by the Scottish nobility.[66] This marriage subsequently led to her resigning the Scottish throne in favour of her infant son, James, and fleeing to England, throwing herself on the mercy of Elizabeth. Queen Elizabeth I was unable to help Mary, supposedly due to her possible involvement in Darnley's death, so therefore kept her cousin captive in a series of castles and fortified houses in England for the next nineteen years.

Contemporary portrait of the Queen of Scots. (Library of Congress, LC-USZ62-121212)

Mary's continuing imprisonment made her a figurehead for factions conspiring against Elizabeth, and Mary, despite her incarceration, continued to be involved in various plots and conspiracies. The final stroke that sealed her fate was her involvement in the Babington Plot of 1586. This scheme, headed by Anthony Babington, ultimately failed due to the leaders being exposed by double agents.[67] Letters were found from Mary to Babington encouraging the plot, which led to her being tried for treason, and she was ultimately found guilty. Her execution took place on 8 February 1587 at Fotheringhay Castle in Northamptonshire.

Mary had always been fond of dogs. Her time in France was reportedly spent in the company of twenty-two lapdogs,[68] so it is only fitting that at the end of her life one of her companions would be by her side. When Mary was led to the hall where her execution would take place, unbeknownst to those present her Skye terrier was hiding underneath the large skirt of her dress. After she was beheaded, her dress began moving, almost as if her body were trying to stand. Upon closer examination, her beloved dog was found shaking and clinging to his mistress's garments. The dog, covered in Mary's blood and sitting between her body and head, refused to leave. Eventually it was forcibly removed, washed and given food, but it refused to eat and, pining for its mistress, died shortly afterwards.

Above: A Portrait of Mary with an image of her execution beneath. (Wellcome Library, London)

Left: A black Skye terrier puppy. Mary's was found hiding underneath her skirts after her execution. (Toloubaev Stanislav)

19 | Dogs in Shakespeare

Dogs have long been used as metaphors to describe determination, loyalty and tenacity. William Shakespeare too uses these descriptions, but also describes dogs in relation to their role in war and fighting, and his writings have formed a key part of our study of the English language, theatre and the arts, and Tudor history.

Contemporary engraving of a dog and boar. (Flikr Commons)

William Shakespeare was born in 1564 in Stratford-upon-Avon. Very little is known about his early life. His marriage to Anne Hathaway was recorded in 1582 and the birth of his three children, Susanna and the twins Hamnet and Judith, are some of the only records of his private life. The absence of records continues to fuel suspicion over how many of the works that are attributed to Shakespeare he actually wrote. He spent time in London where he worked as an actor as well as a writer in the popular theatres of Elizabethan London. Most of his plays were written in the period between 1590 and 1613 while he was in London or touring with his playing company, the Lord Chamberlain's Men. The company subsequently became known as The King's Men on the accession of James I (1603–25) to the throne.

He wrote tragedies, comedies and history plays, along with a number of poems and sonnets. *Julius Caesar*, his play about the Roman emperor, is considered one of Shakespeare's tragedies and in its lines can be found arguably one of the most famous quotes about dog symbolism. In Act 3, Scene 1, the play's namesake has just been murdered when Mark Antony enters. After the others have left him, he delivers a long soliloquy ending with the lines:

… All pity choked with custom of fell deeds;
And Caesar's spirit, ranging for revenge,
With Ate by his side come hot from hell,
Shall in these confines with a monarch's voice
Cry Havoc and let slip the dogs of war,

That this foul deed shall smell above the earth
With carrion men groaning for burial.

Here, dogs are used as a metaphor for mindless and indiscriminate killers who will do simply as their masters order. They also represent those who seek revenge despite the violence that will prevail as a consequence.

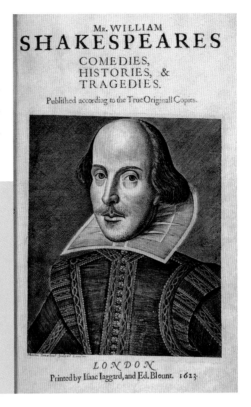

Julius Caesar is thought to have been written in around 1599 and first printed in 1623. None of Shakespeare's original manuscripts survive, so it is the early editions of his plays that form the basis of the study of his work. Some printings even show changes in the text of other famous lines, revealing the tweaks that Shakespeare himself made during his lifetime: 'To be, or not to be, that is the question' from Act 3, Scene 1 of Hamlet only appears as such in 1605, whereas in a 1603 version it appears as 'To be, or not to be, I there's the point'.[69]

Shakespeare's First Folio. (British Library, G.11631, title page)

Shakespeare returned to Stratford in 1613, retiring from his career aged 49. He died on 23 April 1616, aged 52. His two surviving daughters both had children, however Shakespeare's grandchildren died without heirs, therefore ending his direct bloodline.

The use of the famous description of 'the dogs of war' has now become synonymous with many different ideas, but most notably the Frederick Forsyth book *Dogs of War* and subsequent film. The image of the dogs of war as being unscrupulous and violent with no considerations of the outcomes of their actions became attached to the portrayal of human mercenaries, hence the use of the phrase by Forsyth.

2016 marked the 400th year of William Shakespeare's death and commemorations were made all around Britain.

20 | 'The Four-legged Cavalier'

The Parliamentarians and the Royalists formed the opposing sides of the English Civil War. They were also known as Roundheads and Cavaliers. A series of battles made up the war between 1641–51 and the conflict was split into three main phases with three outcomes. The first was the trial and execution of Charles I (1600–49), the second was the exile of his son Charles II (1630–85) and the third was the creation of Britain's first Commonwealth.

Prince Rupert of the Rhine. (Georgios Kollidas, Shutterstock)

It is the first of the three phases of the English Civil War (1642–46) that we are concerned with here. During this period was the Battle of Marston Moor, which was a Parliamentarian victory. On 2 July 1644 the battle was fought by Parliamentarians (Roundheads), led by Lord Fairfax and the Earl of Manchester, and the Royalists (Cavaliers), led by Prince Rupert of the Rhine along with the Marquess of Newcastle.

Prince Rupert was the son of Charles I's sister Elizabeth, making him nephew to the king. Rupert was an excellent cavalry officer and saw service in the Thirty Years War, where he was captured after poor intelligence led him and his men into the main enemy force. During his confinement in Austria, he was visited by Lord Arundel who brought him a dog to keep him company. The dog was named Boye and is described as a white poodle. Boye was always near his master, whatever he was doing, and also found a friend in Charles I, another dog lover.

Prince Rupert was put in charge of the cavalry and Boye, as usual, accompanied his master on the battlefield. His white coat made him easily recognisable, and the troops knew that wherever Boye was, Rupert would

be close. This boosted their morale and helped them to rally around the prince and Boye. Many spectacular victories were won by Rupert and the Cavalier troops, and rumours started to flourish about Boye. One claimed he was in fact an agent of the devil and had magical powers to sneak into Roundhead camps at night invisible and discover information about their movements. The Parliamentarians began to fear Boye and his powers.

Boye became a target for the Roundheads and on Marston Moor, Rupert lost the battle and his faithful friend. A decisive victory for the Roundheads saw Oliver Cromwell emerge as the leading military figure and, with around 8,000 killed or captured, a vast number of the Cavalier forces was lost, as well as the North of England.

How Boye was killed is not exactly clear, but it is said he was found with multiple bullet and stab wounds. This is evidence that the parliamentary troops desperately wanted to make sure he was dead and rejoiced greatly in his passing, producing drawings and poems to celebrate.

21 | The Gravity of the Situation

The comfort and companionship of a dog is never underestimated by owners who have been reassured by the solace and peace of a friend who cares without judgement or words. Leading scientists are no different in this respect and have often found great support in the silent friendship that their dogs give them, many of whom are found within these pages. Not all, however, can be attributed with solving problems of great importance alongside their pensive masters, but instead have a reputation of hindering the progress of great works.

Isaac Newton (1642–1727), leading physicist and mathematician, is perhaps most memorable for his discovery of the laws of gravity, as described in the story of the apple falling from a tree in the orchard at his home in Woolsthorpe, Lincolnshire. Although this was one of Newton's greatest discoveries, it is the counter-factual discoveries or 'what ifs' which concern us here.

Newton was a dog lover and it is suggested that his favourite was a dog named Diamond. Her breed is not known, but she is mostly depicted in images as being a small white, terrier-type dog. She has the dubious reputation of being an 'enemy' of science, as it is said she carelessly knocked over a lit candle in Newton's study, setting fire to the papers strewn across his desk. History does not confirm what it was that Newton had been working on, or how long it took him to replace his findings – if he ever did. We will never know if Newton had been working on a theory that because of Diamond's actions took years or perhaps decades longer to be discovered.

Most accounts say that Diamond destroyed years of work. However, for most dogs such clumsiness is one of their more lovable characteristics. While many of us have never been in the situation of losing years of scientifically important work, we know that staying mad at our family, more especially our dogs, is virtually impossible – a law which Newton himself could probably agree with.

Opposite: Isaac Newton. (Wellcome Library, London)

Below: The fire in Newton's study. (Morel)

22 | Pugs

While it is generally accepted that the pug breed originates from the Orient, its more specific source has always been a matter of speculation. Their journey to Europe is likely to have been through the Dutch East India Company as early as the sixteenth century and whether they were bought, bartered for or stolen, they arrived in Holland and from there travelled to the rest of Europe.

Opposite: Artist's impression of a pug dog. (Mary Evans Picture Library)

Below: The artist William Hogarth (1697–1764) with a pet pug. (Mary Evans Picture Library)

The breed cemented its legendary role in history when, in 1572, a pug named Pompey saved the Prince of Orange, known as William the Silent, from an ambush by the Spanish in Hermingy, France. The story was recalled by Sir Roger Williams' work *Action in the Low Countries*, which was published in 1618.

It was night-time and the prince was sleeping in his tent when Pompey heard the approach of strangers and tried to wake the prince. He began to bark, but to no avail, so the dog jumped on his master and began to paw at his face. This finally woke William and he had just enough time to mount his horse and escape before the Spanish ambush was upon him.

After this, the pug became the official dog of the House of Orange and when William (grandson of William the Silent) and Mary accepted the British throne in 1689, legend has it that in their cortège were numerous pugs wearing orange collars to denote their affiliation with the House of Orange. Therefore they became popular in England, replacing the King Charles spaniels of the previous two monarchs, and were still the favourites of royalty in the nineteenth century. Queen Victoria and her family had many pugs, including Minka, Venus, Ronney and Fatima.

Unfortunately historians now disagree about whether the dog that saved William the Silent was in fact a pug, or a similar Dutch breed.

"ora Model"   F·T·DAWS·

As testament to the loyal characteristic of the breed, an Order of the Pug – which, although it has no connection with ownership of the breed, took its name due to its characteristics of loyalty, steadfastness and trustworthiness – began in Germany around 1740 as a Catholic masonic society. Members were called 'mops', as this is the German word for a pug.

Above: An 1804 engraving of two pugs. (Wellcome Library, London)

Below: A 'grumble' of pug puppies. (Dancestrokes, Shutterstock)

A Victorian illustration of a pug, showing the early look of the breed. (British Library, HMNTS 11651.i.45)

23 | Spaniels

The spaniel breeds are large in number and historically were even larger in the variety of different breeds. In this section, those recognised by The Kennel Club and in existence today will be discussed. A separate section will cover those spaniel lines now extinct. These dogs are well known for their friendly and energetic nature and are always ready to please, making them perfect pets for families.

In terms of grouping the different types of spaniels, they fall into the obvious role of gun dogs but also as toy dogs. As gun dogs they have been use over the centuries for startling hidden game into the open for hunting.

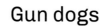

Young English cocker spaniel. (Eric Isselee, Shutterstock)

Gun dogs

The most popular of the spaniels is the cocker spaniel, which was recognised as a separate breed soon after the formation of The Kennel Club. Like many other spaniels, the cocker spaniel is identifiable by its long ears, and originally had a role in flushing out woodcock from hedgerows.

The Sussex spaniel is an old breed that, despite its heritage, is very rarely seen, even in Sussex. He is larger than most other spaniels and has a lovely golden liver-coloured coat.

The field spaniel has much shorter ears than both the cocker and English breeds and is actually a cross between the cocker and the Sussex springer. The breed nearly became extinct twice due to changing fashions in the early 1900s and also the mid-twentieth century.

The English springer spaniel got its name from the way it caused birds to spring in to the air, making them targets

for shooting. The breed only became known by its present name at the turn of the nineteenth century and had previously been known as the Norfolk spaniel. A Welsh springer spaniel is also recognised and forms part of the gun dog group.

The Irish water spaniel, as its name suggests, loves the water and is in fact the tallest of all the spaniels. Its dark-coloured coat is curled like a poodle and this spaniel is different from the others in that its ringlet coat doesn't cover his muzzle or tail. The Irish water spaniel competes in field trials as a retriever but as a spaniel in the show ring.

The Clumber spaniel originates from France but was brought to Britain by the Duke of Newcastle and bred at his home, Clumber

Park (resulting in the breed's name). The Clumber spaniel is predominately white and heavier set that most other spaniels.

Toy Group

The King Charles spaniel, and its relation the Cavalier King Charles, clearly have their ancestry linked to that of the Stuart kings Charles I and Charles II. Despite being a much older breed, the Cavalier King Charles spaniel was only acknowledged by the Kennel Club in 1944 when it was revived as a separate breed from the similar King Charles spaniel. The two are very similar-looking but the King Charles has a shorter nose while the Cavalier is larger. These dogs continue to be popular for urban and rural dwellers and make wonderful pets.

Cavalier King Charles puppies. (WilleeCole Photography)

24 | The American War of Independence

The American War of Independence, alternatively known as the American Revolutionary Wars, raged from 1775–83. It was fought over the independence of thirteen British Colonies that had declared themselves as independent from Britain. The war was long and hard-fought, with both sides taking victories. Although the war was fought on American soil, primarily against its British parent, many other nations were involved on both sides. French Naval Support and money finally tipped the balance in favour of the Americans. The forces also included German mercenaries, who fought for the British.

General Howe. (Library of Congress, LC-USZ62-45179)

In a battle on 4 October 1777, the two commanders-in-chief faced each other at Germantown, then near Philadelphia, now a suburb within it. The British commander was General William Howe (1729–1814) whose army had already had successes in the war, such as capturing New York and Philadelphia. His opponent was George Washington, who had been the head of the Continental Army since May 1775 and after the war became the first President of the United States.

The British had recently captured Philadelphia, which was then the capital of the revolutionaries. The battle at Germantown was a victory for the British – just. However, it also served as a positive reinforcement for the Americans as it is thought that this battle is what persuaded the French to send reinforcements.

It has been surmised that General Howe sympathised on some level with the rebels. Historians usually comment that Howe didn't press his advantage against them, especially after the battle at Germantown. This theory is difficult to prove; however, after the following story it makes sense to many.

George Washington. (Everett Historical, Shutterstock)

After the battle, a dog of a terrier type, possibly a fox terrier, was found near the American lines and thought to be a stray or a displaced inhabitant of the town. On closer inspection it was found that this dog belonged to General Howe, his name appearing on the dog's collar. Upon this discovery the dog was taken to General Washington to decide what should be done. Ideas abounded about keeping the dog as a mascot or trophy to annoy the British but Washington was steadfast in his decision to return the dog.[70] It is said that Washington was also a dog lover and knew the sorrow that separation could cause an owner, his own dog having been sent home to Mount Vernon for safety.[71]

After Washington fed and cared for the dog himself, he gave it to an officer with orders to return it to the British lines. A note was tucked into the dog's collar, which purportedly read:

General Washington's compliments to General Howe. General Washington does himself the pleasure to return to him a dog, which accidentally fell into his hands, and, by the inscription on the collar, appears to belong to General Howe.[72]

It is heart-warming to think that even in the midst of a war that tore Britain and America apart there was still occasion to be gentlemanly. Two dog lovers, who found themselves on opposite sides of the war could still appreciate the comfort a dog can bring.

General Howe resigned his command of the army in late 1777, which was accepted in 1778, and he returned home. It would be easy to speculate that he no longer wished to fight the gentleman who returned his dog to him, although other reasons are most likely the cause.

Walter Scott (1771–1832)

To most modern audiences, the name Walter Scott is sadly of no consequence. However, he was a Scottish writer of plays, poems and novels whose works are famous all over the world, and include *Rob Roy* and *Ivanhoe*. He was a prolific writer who was extremely popular to his contemporaries. Among his literary credentials, Scott also found the missing 'Honours Of Scotland' through his literary interest in historical stories. For this he was granted the title of baronet.

Walter Scott pictured with one of his beloved pets. (Library of Congress, LC-DIG-pga-07782)

In 1825 Britain suffered from a banking crisis, based on speculative investments made on the stock market. This hit Scott hard as the publishing business, in which he had a commercial interest, folded, meaning he owed huge sums to creditors. However, instead of taking money from friends, he put his property and income from his works in the hands of those creditors in order to pay his debt through his past and future literary contributions.

His son-in-law, John Lockhart, wrote a biography of Scott after his death which is considered by some to be the most famous biography in the English language after James Boswell's *Life of Samuel Johnson*. In this biography, Lockhart published many of Scott's letters, which gave an insight into the man himself.

An account of Scott described him as the 'greatest dog-lover' of all the literary men.[73] A letter written by Scott and included in his biography shows his great attachment to his dogs when he thought he might have to leave them due to his financial problems;

My dogs will wait for me in vain. It is foolish – but the thoughts of parting from these dumb creatures have moved me more than any of the painful reflections I have put down. Poor things! I must get them kind masters! There may be yet those who, loving me, may love my dog because it has been mine. I must end these gloomy forebodings, or I shall lose the tone of mind with which men should meet distress. I feel my dogs' feet on my knees – I hear them whining and seeking me everywhere. This is nonsense but it is what they would do could they know how things may be.[74]

Scott's favourite dog was reputedly called Camp. Lockhart wrote in the biography that at one time he was the 'constant parlour dog'. The dog was very handsome, very intelligent and naturally very fierce, but gentle as a lamb among the children.[75] He goes on to say that Scott always talked to Camp as if he understood what was being said, something many of us are guilty of. Lockhart also wrote of the sorrow Camp's death caused his father-in-law:

Above: The Dandie Dinmont, named after a dog owner in one of Scott's books. (Eric Isselee, Shutterstock)

Opposite: Walter Scott. (Library of Congress, LC-DIG-ppmsc-07693)

He was buried on a fine moonlight night, in the little garden behind the house in Castle Street, immediately opposite the window at which Scott usually sat writing. My wife told me that she remembered the whole family standing in tears about the grave as her father himself smoothed down the turf above Camp, with the saddest expression of face she had ever seen in him. He had been engaged to dine abroad that day, but apologised on account of the death of a dear old friend[76]

Another fact worth mentioning in relation to Scott's writings, apart from the many dogs that littered his works, is his involvement in the naming of the breed known as the Dandie Dinmont. In his book *Guy Mannering* of 1815, the character Dandie Dinmont was a Border farmer who had many terrier dogs. The dogs in the novel were all called 'Mustard' or 'Pepper' because of their colouring.[77] In reality the breed's colours are mustard or pepper, and therefore the dogs in the novel were identified by contemporaries as being the same breed, and they subsequently became known by this name.

26 | Lord Byron (1788–1824)

Lord Byron's devotion to his dogs is something many pet owners can probably appreciate and, given Byron's qualities and standing, would replicate in verse and stone themselves if possible. Although Byron had many dogs during his lifetime, a Newfoundland named Boatswain touched him most deeply. When this dog died he was moved to build a memorial, which still attracts visitors today, not only to view the tomb but also to reflect upon the compassion and companionship between humans and their pets.

Lord Byron. (Everett Historical, Shutterstock)

Anecdotes about Boatswain show the intelligence and caring nature of the dog. One such tale recounts the somewhat tense relationship between Boatswain and Mrs Byron's dog, Gilpin, a fox terrier. The quarrelling pair were always fighting, sometimes so ferociously that it was thought that they would do each other harm, so Gilpin was sent to live with a tenant at Newstead. All was quiet in the house once more and when Lord Byron left to study at Cambridge, Boatswain was left in the charge of a servant. However, one morning Boatswain had disappeared and could not be found until later that evening when he arrived home, accompanied by Gilpin. Boatswain escorted his new-found friend to the kitchen for food, whereupon he commence to lick him. Boatswain had gone to fetch his former foe in order to return him to his house; the two no longer quarrelled and instead Boatswain became Gilpin's protector in many subsequent battles against other dogs.[78] It is perhaps no wonder that Byron was so dedicated to Boatswain.

In 1808 Boatswain contracted rabies while fighting with a cur in Mansfield. Byron purportedly nursed him and, while at first unaware of the dog's affliction, more than once wiped the foam from Boatswain's mouth with his bare hand until he died.[79] Byron wrote to a friend afterwards, saying, 'Boatswain is dead! – he expired in a state of madness on the 18th, after suffering much, yet retaining all the gentleness of his nature to the last, never attempting to do the least injury to any one near him.'[80]

Landseer Newfoundland, like Boatswain. (Erik Lam, Shutterstock)

Byron erected a monument to Boatswain in the gardens of Newstead Abbey with the following inscription on one of its sides:

Near this spot
Are deposited the Remains of one
Who possessed Beauty without Vanity,
Strength without Insolence,
Courage without Ferocity,
And all the virtues of Man without his Vices.
This Praise, which would be unmeaning Flattery
If inscribed over human ashes,
Is but a just tribute to the Memory of
BOATSWAIN, a Dog,
Who was born in Newfoundland, May, 1803
And died at Newstead, November 18. 1808

In a will made in 1811, Byron directed that he was to be buried in a vault near the monument to Boatswain. However, at the time of his death Byron no longer owned Newstead Abbey, having sold it to Thomas Wildman in 1818, and Byron was never interred at the spot he had preferred.[81]

Boatswain's memorial as it appeared at the turn of the twentieth century. (British Library, 000056737)

27 | British Bulldog

The bulldog is undoubtedly a British classic, most notably connected to the stubborn and unyielding attitude of the British public, especially during wartime. Images of this breed have been used on wartime posters to depict the British people and it is unsurprisingly considered the national dog. Its association with John Bull, the quintessential British man, has meant the breed has been commercially recognisable and appeared on dog-related products such as dog food and even cigars, but also lends its name to planes such as the Bristol bulldog of the late 1920s.

An original seventeenth-century engraving of a bull and a bulldog doing battle, showing how the breed has changed over the centuries. (Wellcome Library, London)

The breed has changed over the centuries, with its features becoming more prominent, such as its short legs and face, but it is one of our oldest indigenous breeds. The original purpose of the breed, as suggested by its name, was bull-baiting.

John Caius, a sixteenth-century author, wrote a large manuscript devoted to the dogs of England in which he describes a dog that sounds very similar to the bulldog. The name under which he describes this dog is 'Bandogge' which had the following characteristics: heavy body, frightful to behold, fierce and used, amongst other things, for bull-bating. Caius goes on to describe the dog as courageous yet violent, with the ability to strike fear into the hearts of men, but that the breed itself has no fear.[82] In 1800 little had changed, and Thomas Bewick wrote in his *General History of Quadrupeds*

Modern British bulldogs, young and old. (WilleeCole Photography, Shutterstock)

that the breed 'is the fiercest of all the dog kind, and is probably the most courageous creature in the world'.[83]

The outward image of the breed today belies the loyalty, humour and good nature of its character.

ALL BRITISH

"A tough customer."

Above: Original First World War postcard showing a bulldog as a British soldier.

Left: A beautiful painted bulldog postcard from just before the First World War; the caption reads 'All British'.

28 | Dogfighting

Bull- and bear-baiting had been a popular sport since the Roman period, when dogs were often pitted against other animals in the Colosseum. This trend was continued through to the Tudor period and a number of bear gardens were built in London to house the bears and other beasts that would take part in these events.

Dogs were selectively bred for the role that they carried out and the bulldog's name obviously betrays the purpose for the development of the breed. The dogs bred over the centuries, however, do not resemble those we know today, even when they share the same names.

Although bull-baiting is undoubtedly cruel to today's sensibilities, there was a time when it was illegal to slaughter a bull that had not first been baited with dogs. It was thought that baiting the animal first made its meat more tender. Bull-baiting was forbidden under Oliver Cromwell's rule as it allowed men to gather in large groups, which worried him. However, after the Restoration its popularity returned. Badger-digging was also popular, where the dog would attempt to bring the badger out from its sett.

In 1835 the Cruelty to Animals Act was passed which outlawed baiting and therefore ended the sport. However, when bull- and bear-baiting ceased, dog fighting became more popular (though still illegal under the Act) as it required less space and therefore could be done in secret. The height of popularity for dog fighting was between the 1820s and 1830s, when it was seen as a way of providing sport and entertainment as well as competition between rival dog breeders.

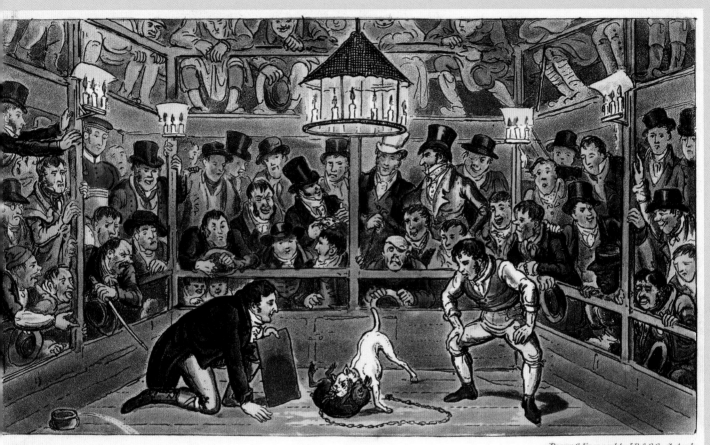

Drawn & Engraved by I.R. & G.Cruikshank.

Tom & Jerry sporting their blunt on the phenomenon Monkey, Jacco Macacco, at the Westminster Pit.

29 | William Wordsworth (1770–1850)

William Wordsworth held the title of Poet Laureate from 1843 until his death in 1850. He is still the only Poet Laureate to not write any official verse while in the position. Although there was no obligation to write, this alteration was made when Wordsworth was given the honour by Prime Minister Peel. At the age of 73 he was also the oldest Laureate. Perhaps Wordsworth's most famous poetic line is 'I wandered lonely as a cloud'; however, he was imbued with affection of canine companions.

Opposite: William Wordsworth. (Everett Historical, Shutterstock)

Below: Dove Cottage, home of Wordsworth. (Andrew Roland, Shutterstock)

In two volumes of poems published in 1807, Wordsworth wrote of a dog he encountered while with friends: 'Incident, characteristic of a favourite Dog, which belonged to a Friend of the Author'.[84] The poem describes four dogs who belong to a master who also cared for sheep and cattle. Two dogs are specified as breeds for scent and two for speed, presumably for hunting. The poem then descends into a description of the dogs in pursuit of a hare. In this fast-paced verse, the thin layer of frost on the river breaks and Dart, one of the greyhounds, plunges into the water. Two of the other dogs, Prince and Swallow, continued on their sport but the fourth dog, Music, stops and loses interest in chasing the hare. Instead she tries to help her canine friend. Without care for her own safety or life, she attempts to save him until he finally sinks beneath the water and appears above it no more.[85]

Through Wordsworth's delicate words, the whole scene from happiness to sorrow is skilfully traversed, taking the reader on the whole journey and the emotions it creates.

30 | Dalmatians

The Dalmatian, with its distinctive spots and film-star looks, has become one of the most easily recognisable breeds. In history, however, the breed had a distinctive role and was a friend to working horses. It was during the Regency period (1811–20) that the breed came to prominence as a carriage dog. Due to the breed's natural athleticism, they were able to cover great distances without tiring, which made them suitable for keeping up with horse-drawn carriages.

The dogs would run alongside or under the horse-drawn carriages, whether they were carrying passengers or goods, and protect them from other dogs who may have run up to the horses and scared them. Horse theft was a problem during this period, resulting in many coachmen having to sleep in the stables with the horses to protect them. However, the Dalmatian was able to keep guard over the horses during the night and warn off any potential thieves. This allowed many coachmen to spend a more restful night in a local inn, with his horses safely guarded by their canine companions.

The role of the Dalmatian working with horses, running with them and also protecting them, is probably why the breed was favoured in many fire stations. Just as with carriages, the dog would run out ahead or with the horses who were pulling the fire engine, protecting them and warning of their approach. When horse-drawn fire engines were replaced with motor engines, many Dalmatians still retained their role running with the engines and now many fire stations around the world have a Dalmatian. In Britain, fire brigades would not necessarily have a Dalmatian, but would have any

An American firehouse Dalmatian mascot. (Tinyfroglet/Flikr)

A young Dalmatian. (Eric Isselee)

breed of dog or even a cat. Nowadays it is mainly in America where Dalmatians will be found in fire stations.

The relationship between dogs and men of the fire service goes back a long way and even phrases used today bear testament to their bond. When a call is received by the fire brigade that needs their immediate attention it is called a 'shout'. The origins of this term are from the early days of the service, when barking dogs would go out in front of the fire engine and the men travelling with the engine would shout to warn people of their approach and hasten their journey through crowded streets.[86]

The fireman's link with animals is long established, with many of their working hours spent saving trapped and injured animals. However, it is not as widely known that rendering humanitarian aid is part of their role and this includes the protection of animals. First-aid courses, including resuscitation of animals, are also part of the training available from the fire service.

A Georgian illustration of a 'coach dog'. (Wellcome Library, London)

The breed has undoubtedly been made famous by Walt Disney's animated adaptation of the story of *The Hundred and One Dalmatians* in 1961. Remakes, including a live action film, have been made since, showing the popularity of the story. The original novel was written by British author and playwright Dorothy 'Dodie' Smith in 1956.

31 | Charles Dickens (1812–58)

Charles Dickens' stories are still loved the world over and studied by students of English literature and history. Favourites like *Oliver Twist* are performed everywhere from the West End to schools all over Britain.

Dickens was born on 7 February 1812 in Portsmouth and had a difficult and turbulent upbringing, many incidents forming the stories and characters he would pen as an adult. He is one of the most iconic Victorian figures, and his life as well as his works have been of public interest. For example, his relationship with his mistress and his separation from his wife, Catherine Hogarth, are well documented. Dickens had many dogs himself, so it is unsurprising that he would write them into his books.

Charles Dickens in his study at Gads Hill. Everett Historical, Shutterstock)

Charles Dickens. (Library of Congress, LC-USZ61-694)

One of Dickens' most classic works is *Oliver Twist*. It is the tale of a boy whose life begins badly, and who is cared for terribly in the workhouse before living on the streets in a gang of boys led by Fagin, in which all comes right in the end. His second novel, this was a story much like Dickens' own. In this story, Bull's-eye, the dog owned by Bill Sikes, truly exemplifies the idea of dogs taking after their owners. The dog is portrayed as a vicious and mean dog, much like Sikes, who is treated badly by his master. The connection between the two characters is continued to their ends where, despite Bill's attempts to rid himself of the dog, thinking that it would betray that he is Nancy's murderer, the dog continues to be a reminder and embodiment of his guilt.

David Copperfield was another serialised novel that wasn't published in book form until 1850. The story is thought to be the most closely based on Dickens' own life and follows the eponymous character through his youth into an adult. After the trials and tribulations of his early life, David marries Dora Spenlow, who has a lapdog named Jip. Dora is very attached to this dog and fusses over it constantly.

There are many other examples in Dickens' work, but these are probably the most famous.

32 | Chance, the Fire Station Dog

Though not a Dalmatian like original carriage and fire-engine dogs, and in fact most likely to have been a mongrel, the popularity of one of London's fire dogs shows the interest and appeal of dogs in society. It is unlikely that Chance was the first fire dog, although he is probably the first to receive the fame of being painted and having his obituary in many London papers.

Chance was observed at fires where the London Fire Establishment men were present, and it seemed that he preferred their grey uniforms to the other private fire brigades of the time, as he refused to follow any other. It is written that Chance rotated among all of the separate stations operated by the London Brigade and made friends of all the firemen, so that he was well known to all. He also became a recognisable figure when the brigade was called out as he would follow the fire engine and even enter burning buildings, treating them as a playground, as well as enjoying a bath in the water jets.

Chance the fireman's dog.
(© London Fire Brigade/
Mary Evans Picture Library)

Eventually his original owner, a weaver from Spitalfields, heard about his dog from the newspaper reports, came to fetch him and returned him to his home. However, Chance continued to return to the fire station and his owner finally gave him up to the firemen. He was given a brass collar, which the firemen had engraved with the words:

Stop me not, but let me jog,
I'm the Fire Establishment dog.

THE WHITEFRIARS FIRE ENGINE
AND ITS FAMOUS DOG "BARON"

Some original newspaper reports describe Chance as a black-and-tan terrier-type dog. Chance was even in attendance when the Houses of Parliament burned down in October 1834, when a print was produced of him running around in the confusion.

Chance suffered many injuries in the course of his role: his forelegs were run over by the fire engine, he suffered burns to his face and sustained an injury caused by a bystander who kicked him in the jaw. However, Chance was expertly cared for by the firemen of the London Establishment until his death on 10 October 1835. He remained faithful to the last, as just hours before his death the fire bell rang and as the engine departed Chance rose from his bed and tried to follow it, only to collapse at the door to the fire station. In honour of their faithful companion, men from the brigade subscribed to have Chance stuffed in order to mount a memorial at the Central Station in Watling Street.[87]

The case that housed Chance was to have a scroll inscribed, 'Chance, well known as the firemen's dog, died Oct. 10. 1835. This is humbly inscribed to the Committee of the London Fire Establishment, by their obedient servants.'[88] Unfortunately, the taxidermist who was to preserve Chance found the dog's celebrity to be a greater source of income and instead of giving him back to the firemen, sold him to a showman who admitted visitors to see Chance for a penny a time. A fireman who happened to be admitted saw the missing dog, left and returned with more firemen who reclaimed Chance and displayed him at the central station.[89]

Opposite: Baron, the Whitefriars fire dog, runs alongside the fire engine, performing the same role as Chance. (Mary Evans Picture Library)

Below: A Georgian fire-team pictured in action. (British Library, 190.e.1, 35)

33 | Florence Nightingale's Inspiration

Florence Nightingale (1820–1910) is well known as the 'lady of the lamp' who cared for wounded and sick soldiers during the Crimean War (1853–56) at a hospital based in Scutari, Constantinople (now Istanbul). Florence, named after the Italian city where she was born, had a very privileged upbringing. She was well educated and lived on the large estates that belonged to her family. Her choice to become a nurse, a profession not befitting a lady of her status, was a shock to her family and friends. At this point in history, nurses were generally unskilled and performed only basic tasks, so it was a profession deemed suitable for lower-class women. However, Florence's resolve to pursue this career is said to have stemmed from a vision she had in February 1837.

Florence Nightingale doing her rounds. (Wellcome Library, London)

A few days before this vision, Florence had been out riding with a friend when they came across a man named Roger, who was a shepherd, near to one of Florence's family homes.[90] Roger was normally accompanied by a sheepdog named Cap who helped him to round up the sheep, but on this occasion Cap was missing and Florence asked after him. Roger explained that Cap had been sleeping outside his cottage when a group of boys had thrown stones at the dog and as he got up to go inside one of the stones hit his leg and he was subsequently unable to put it to the floor or walk on it. Roger said he would have to return to the cottage later to put Cap to sleep as he couldn't afford to keep a dog who could not work.[91]

Florence was upset to think that Cap would die so she decided to visit him along with her companion. They found Cap in the cottage and, on seeing Florence, he attempted to greet her. Florence's

companion looked at Cap's leg and told her that the leg was not broken and just badly bruised, and that with the use of hot bandages to sooth the bruising and aid the healing he would be as right as rain in no time. Florence proceeded to light a fire in order to boil some water and prepare the bandages, bathing Cap's paw. On leaving the cottage, they saw Roger, who was returning with means to kill Cap. They explained that he would recover in a couple days after some care and rest.[92]

A few days later, Florence again saw Roger tending to his sheep. Cap ran to her, still limping, but much happier to be in the company of Roger and his sheep. It was soon after this event that Florence had the dream that would change her life, many hundreds of soldiers' lives and the nursing profession forever.

34 | Dog Thieves

The thought of a beloved pet being lost is unbearable, therefore the idea of stealing one from another owner is completely incomprehensible.

However, dog thieves found a great deal of work in Victorian London, in the fashionable and upper-class neighbourhoods of Belgravia, Chelsea and Knightsbridge. The dogs most targeted were pets with wealthy owners who would pay their ransom or breeds of high value whose resale would be assured. Breeds such as Newfoundlands, Poodles and ladies' lapdogs were sought, as well as sporting dogs such as setters and retrievers, which were favoured by such criminals.

The modus operandi would be as follows:

Poodles, one of the most popular types of dog to steal in historic London. (British Library, C.58.cc.1.)

POODLES.

> ... when they see a handsome dog with a lady or gentleman they follow it and see where the person resides. So soon as they have ascertained this they loiter about the house for days with a piece of liver prepared by a certain process, and soaked in some ingredient which dogs are uncommonly fond of. They are so partial to it that they will follow the stranger some distance in preference to following their master. The thieves generally carry small pieces of this to entice the dog away with them, when they seize hold of it in a convenient place, and put it into a bag they carry with them.[93]

There was, however, another level to these devious affairs. After the dogs had been procured, especially ones who had wealthy owners, they would be passed to a 'receiver' who would look after them for a time; this was often just enough for a 'dog-finder' to take on the task of finding the lost dog for a sizeable fee. These receivers and finders were often linked to the thieves in a network designed to extort money from the dog owner.

There are many examples from national newspapers of owners placing classified ads in the hope of being reunited with their lost dogs. In 1786 a classified ad was placed in *The Times* by an owner who had lost their brown-and-white spaniel, with a half-guinea reward offered. However, a warning was also given thus that 'no other reward will be offered, nor will he be advertised anymore; and whoever is found secreting him, will be prosecuted'[94]. The name of this dog was Rover. Another, not dissimilar, tale was printed and disseminated around Chichester in West Sussex in 1745. A small flyer was produced describing a dog that had gone missing from the Goodwood Estate, which is now famous for racing of both horses and cars. The dog was owned by a Mr Peckham Williams and was seen last in the area with a 'ragged fellow', who it was thought had stolen the canine. This dog was also named Rover, which seems to have been popular around this time and is not perhaps as modern as we may think.[95]

A Sunday morning dog fair at Bethnal Green, London, where stolen dogs were often sold. (Mary Evans Picture Library)

The problem of dog theft has been a consistent one and even in Georgian times cases were heard at high-level courts, including one which was heard at the Court of King's Bench in the Guildhall, London that concerned two men who considered themselves the rightful master of the same pug. The defendant admitted stealing the dog; however he alleged that he had been the original owner and was as such simply recovering his dog. The lord chief justice who heard the case suggested that it be settled out of court, otherwise the evidence of the dog would probably be needed. The defence lawyer agreed with the judge – the dog was his leading witness.

THE STREET DOG-SELLER.

In 1844, the increasing problem of dog theft resulted in a petition being given to Parliament to intervene: the outcome was for a select committee to investigate, which was unfortunately viewed as farcical in the press. In justifying the need for the investigation, the Honourable H.T. Liddell stated that at that time 'no man's dog was safe'.

So, even though the bond between man and dog has been unbreakable for thousands of years, the relationship has not always been honoured by our fellow man.

Opposite: A London street seller trading dogs. (Mary Evans Picture Library)
Above: Selling stolen dogs on the street in Victorian London.

Charles Darwin's Dog

Not all dogs need to have committed brave acts or notable feats in order to warrant a mention in history. Some are noteworthy for their friendship and companionship to those who have been prominent scientists or explorers. One example of this can be found in Charles Darwin's dog.

Below, right: Polly, Charles Darwin's dog, posing for Darwin's last book on expressions in animals and men. (Wellcome Library, London)

Below: Charles Darwin. (Library of Congress, LC-USZ62-52389)

In *The Life and Letters of Charles Darwin*, his son Francis discussed some of the everyday parts of his father's life: 'My father was always fond of dogs, and as a young man had the power of stealing away the affections of his sister's pets ... In my memory there were only two dogs which had much connection with my father ... a large black and white half-bred retriever, called Bob ... but the dog most closely associated with my father was ... Polly.'

Polly was a white rough-haired fox terrier that Charles Darwin loved. 'He was delightfully tender to Polly, and never showed any impatience at the attentions she required ... She died, or rather had to be killed, a few days after his death.' Francis' final mention of Polly was to say that his father was 'always rejoiced to get home ... he used greatly to enjoy the welcome he got from his dog Polly, who would get wild with excitement, panting, squeaking, rushing round the room, and jumping on and off the chairs; and he used to stoop down, pressing her face to his, letting her lick him, and speaking to her with a peculiarly tender caressing voice.'

Finally, to conclude with Darwin's own thoughts on dogs, his book *The Expression of the Emotion in Man and Animals* of 1872 states that 'man himself cannot express love and humility by external signs, so plainly as does a dog, when with drooping ears, hanging lips, flexuous body, and wagging tail, he meets his beloved master'.

36 | Preston Park

Just inside the modern city of Brighton and Hove lies Preston Park, a large green space with its manor house sitting at the northern end. There are two reasons why this property is special in its commemoration of its canine inhabitants, both inside and outside.

The house is open to visitors and is still furnished as it was when the Stanford family occupied it. On the inside, adorning the stairs, hang portraits of many of the family dogs. These range from British classics such as Yorkshire terriers to oriental breeds such as the Pekingese. Others, throughout the house in paint and porcelain, show the family love of dogs with many depictions in both artwork and photographs.

Preston Manor entrance hall. (Royal Pavilion & Museums Brighton & Hove)

Outside, many of those animals pictured inside are commemorated in the small pet cemetery found within the walled garden, where many of the stones have worn away after the many years in the garden and are in desperate need of conservation. Although the dogs found inside Preston Manor are mainly the pets of the last Stanford family members to occupy the house, the cemetery outside is actually much older and can be traced to Eleanor Macdonald.

Eleanor had remarried after the death of her first husband, William Stanford, in 1853.

She had three daughters from this marriage: Flora and twins named Diana and Christiana (known as Lily). Eleanor and the twins were responsible for the creation of the cemetery,[96] which was continued by Ellen Thomas-Stanford.

As laid out in the will of Ellen and Charles Thomas-Stanford, the contents of the house, the gardens and the building itself passed to the Corporation of Brighton and was first opened to the public in October 1933.[97] The first curator of the house was Henry Roberts and his daughter Margery had an interest in the small cemetery in the garden.

In March 1935 Margery wrote an article in the *Sussex Daily News*. She discussed each headstone in turn and offered many anecdotal stories about the dogs. Unfortunately a great deal of information about the tombs had been lost over the years by the time Margery wrote the article, but her work has undoubtedly created a historical record for the benefit of future generations.

The identifiable gravestones gave the names of the following dogs: Pickle, Fritz, Peter, Tatters, Soot, Beauty, Queenie, Punch, Jim, Tiny, Jock, Kylin and another Peter. Many stories, as well as the epitaphs on their graves, were recorded by Margery:

Fritz died in April 1892 and was Miss MacDonald's Dachshund who liked to bark at men. This included male servants and visitors.

A Scotch terrier called Peter is next to Fritz and apparently had a similarly grumpy disposition. His gravestone reads:

In memory of dear Peter, who was cross and sulky, but loved us. Died December 1886.

Peter reportedly disliked anyone in an apron, even if worn by one of the family!

A beautifully simple epitaph can be found on one of the other stones about which even Margery had no further information. It simply reads:

Here Lies Tatters, Not that it much matters, 1884.

Not all the dogs were inhabitants of Preston Manor and one stone marks the grave of 'Tiny, Lady Hill's Little Pet Dog'. The dog had accompanied his mistress to the manor on 15 May 1886. The next dog, Jock, was an Airedale who had come from Edwin Richardson, a person of great interest throughout her book, and made an excellent house dog. His stone reads, 'Jock. Stout of Heart and Body. 1911–1919.' Kylin was a Pekingese belonging to Mrs Thomas-Stanford and, although she was indifferent to people, loved the company of other dogs. Jock and she were great friends. 'Faithful and Fearless' adorns her stone.[98]

In total there are at least sixteen dogs and a handful of cats known to be buried in this cemetery, which can be seen by any visitor to Preston Manor, as the gardens are freely open. If you are lucky, sometimes a tour is organised by the extremely knowledgeable Paula Wrightson, who inspired me with such fantastic information on one such tour.

Lilas Porteous in June 1907 aged 11 sitting on the stairs in the garden of Preston Manor with a boxer dog. (Royal Pavilion & Museums Brighton & Hove)

37 | Jack the Ripper

Whether you believe in a conspiracy theory or not, the murders attributed to Jack the Ripper were both shocking and horrendous, even to inhabitants used to the debauchery of Victorian London. While there is no need to go into the details of the debate over how many murders were committed, numerous conspiracy theories or the identity of the Ripper himself, it is pertinent to give some context to the events.

In the summer and autumn of 1888 at least six women are thought to have been murdered in the East End by the serial killer. The name 'Jack the Ripper' came from a letter sent to a London news agency supposedly from the killer in which he named himself. Today the validity of these letters is widely contested. They are most often assumed to have been written by hoaxers or the press themselves to increase interest and sales of their newspapers.

Sir Charles Warren, the man who hunted Jack the Ripper.

The six murders which tend to be associated with Jack the Ripper are:

Martha Tabram – 7 August
Polly Nichols – 31 August
Annie Chapman – 8 September
Elizabeth Stride – 30 September
Catherine Eddowes – 30 September
Mary Jane Kelly – 9 November

All these women were prostitutes and as such were accustomed to using the small dark alleys, which were numerous in Whitechapel at this time, to carry out their business. This meant opportunities were numerous to lure an unsuspecting victim to their death.

In October 1888 *The Times*, in an article about the murders, criticised the police investigation for having found no suspects nor discoveries. It does reveal, however, a new technique being used by the desperate investigators: bloodhounds.

Yesterday [October 19th] the police were engaged in an exhaustive search of the ground between the Victoria Embankment and Cannon-row – the site of the new police offices. The purpose of the search was an endeavour to find other parts of the mutilated remains already discovered, an those engaged were assisted by a bloodhound.[99]

An article in 1934 further expanded upon the use of blood-hounds during the investigation. It stated that Sir Charles Warren, the Commissioner of Police at the time of the murders, asked for two dogs to be brought to London. It was observed that during the two months that the dogs were in London the murderer was quiet, the dogs seemingly proving a deterrent.[100]

PUNCH, OR THE LONDON CHARIVARI.—September 22, 1888.

MURDER

BLIND-MAN'S BUFF.

(*As played by the Police.*)

" TURN ROUND THREE TIMES,
AND CATCH WHOM YOU MAY ! "

The famous 1888 cartoon 'Blind Man's Buff'. (British Library)

38 | Queen Victoria

As a monarch, Queen Victoria gave her country nearly the whole of her life and showed a great amount of care for her people and their animals. She had been the longest-reigning monarch in British history, serving sixty-four years, until she was surpassed by Queen Elizabeth II in 2015.

Victoria ruled at the time of the British Empire, when Britain was the greatest power among the countries of the world. Her marriage to Prince Albert produced nine children and influenced many of the royal families of Europe and beyond.

Victoria is known for her fondness of animals, dogs in particular, of which she had many throughout her lifetime. Pictures abound of her and her dogs, and her wider family seems to have inherited this enthusiasm as well. She loved a vast range of breeds, far too many to list, and so only some of which are described below.

Her liking of dogs came at an early age. One of her favourites was named Dash, who was a King Charles spaniel. Dash and Victoria had been together since her childhood, and he continued with her when she became queen. On the day of her coronation in 1838, when the queen returned to Buckingham Palace after the gruellingly long ceremony, the first thing she did was give Dash his bath.

Queen Victoria also had dachshunds at Windsor Palace, undoubtedly because of her connection with Albert, who was from Saxony, now part of modern-day Germany.

The queen also had many Pekingese, the first of which was called Looty and had a royal pedigree of her own, as well as being one of the first of the breed to reach Britain. She was given to the queen by General Dunn and came from the Summer Palace in Peking, left behind when the Imperial household was evacuated during the Second Opium War in 1860. Looty lived until 1872.

Queen Victoria's collie, Oscar.
(Mary Evans Picture Library)

In 1887 the queen's dog Noble, a collie, died at Balmoral. He was buried in the grounds and had his own headstone with an epitaph which read:

Noble by name by nature noble too
faithful companion sympathetic true
His remains are interred here[101]

The queen, like many avid breeders and dog lovers, sent some of her dogs to the Crufts show, including Pomeranians and collies. Her son, the Prince of Wales (the future King Edward VII) sent basset hounds which he had bred himself. Queen Victoria's collie Darnley II won first prize in the open class for dogs of his breed and in 1892 the queen again exhibited at the show with Pomeranians.

Albert was also a lover of dogs and when he came to Britain to marry Victoria he had his greyhound, Eos, brought over. The famous dog painter Sir Edward Landseer was commissioned to paint a portrait of the dog in 1841 and Victoria gave the portrait to her husband as a gift at Christmas the same year. Eos died in 1844 at the age of 10. The queen would have been confident in Landseer's skills as a painter as she had commissioned him before, in 1837, to paint *Her Majesty's Favourite Pets*. This included mainly dogs but also the queen's parrot.

Queen Victoria was also interested in improving the welfare of dogs and gave thought to legislation and progress that could be made. She gave royal status to the Society for the Prevention of Cruelty to Animals, thus creating the RSPCA we know today.

And finally, as a concluding note to the long and fruitful life of one of Britain's greatest monarchs, when she was lying close to death, her Pomeranian was with her, sitting close by on her bed.

The royal pets included dachshunds. (Lee319, Shutterstock)

39 | Dog Carts

Until the beginning of the nineteenth century, dog carts were used throughout England, but especially in London. These carts, pulled by teams of up to five dogs, were employed in transporting goods and often used by butchers to carry their produce to market.[102] These carts caused havoc in the already overcrowded streets of London until legislation was passed to ban their use.

One mid-nineteenth-century description of these carts in London:

In the beginning of the present century many of the butchers' carts in London were drawn by teams of dogs, often five in number. The carts had high wheels, and in the double shafts in front two large dogs were harnessed; three smaller ones ran underneath. They went at high speed, and only appeared in the morning and evening in the streets.[103]

Vintage photograph of a little girl with a dog cart, early twentieth century. (Everett Collection, Shutterstock)

The breeds that were used for this work are thought to have been Newfoundlands and large bulldogs, among others. It is said that the dogs would bark while running, creating excitement and rivalry between other carts.

First they were banned within the Metropolitan area in 1840 (bill passed in 1839) and then throughout the rest of the UK from 1842.

Small notices in *The Times* after the passing of each bill gave notice of the restrictions and enforcement of the law now to be put in place. In 1839 the notice from police read:

After 1st day of January next, 1840, every person, who, within the metropolitan police district, shall use any dog for the purpose of drawing, or helping to draw, any cart, carriage, truck, or barrow, shall be liable to a penalty.

A dog cart pulling a carriage in Belgium at the turn of the century. (Library of Congress, LC-DIG-npcc-32929)

A Flemish milk cart pulled by
dogs. (Library of Congress,
LC-DIG-ppmsc-05620)

In 1842 a similar notice appeared in reference to the bill having been passed to cover the use of dog carts in the rest of the country.

Unfortunately, with dogs no longer able to be used in this manner, there was no need for their masters to keep them and many dogs were let loose to become strays.

40 | Dog Collar Sellers

Henry Mayhew's extensive survey into the life of the inhabitants of London in the 1850s shone a light into the lives of people who had never previously been the focus of such a study. The aim of the multi-volume work was to become 'a cyclopaedia of the industry, the want and the vice of the great Metropolis'.[107] In Mayhew's own words, what made his work very different was the fact that it was a 'history of a people, from the lips of the people themselves':[108] a very early oral history project to capture the thoughts and lives of the people he encountered on the streets of London.

Through his efforts to detail everything about the people of London, he gave us an insight into those who made their living from dogs, or their associated goods. In his first volume, he includes 'The street-seller of dogs' collars'. An illustration of one of these sellers is provided in the book, which shows a man carrying his merchandise around his neck as well as hanging from his arms. We are told that there were twelve regular sellers of this kind at that time, and around a quarter of these were only selling dog collars.

Mayhew thoroughly described the type of collars being sold:

The collars most in demand are brass. One man pointed out to me the merits of his stock, which he retailed from 6d. each (for the very small ones) to 3s. – for collars seemingly big enough for Pyrenean sheep dogs. Some of the street-sold collars have black and red rims and linings; others are of leather, often scarlet, stitched ornamentally over a sort of jointed iron or wire-work. A few are of strong compact steel chain-work; 'but them's more the fashion', said one seller, 'for sporting dogs, like pointers and greyhounds, and is very seldom bought in the streets. It's the pet dogs as is our best friends.'[109]

The income of these street sellers was also obtained by Mayhew. Through his research he perceived that each seller could sell an average of twelve collars a week, making around 12*s*. Mayhew also notes that any good seller will also endeavour to get a name engraved on the collar for 1*d* per letter. So an average of 12*s* weekly income per seller of dog collars, times twelve for the twelve regular sellers, makes £374 (20*s* to a pound) being spent yearly on dog collars bought on the streets of London. Today this would equate to nearly £45,000.[110]

Far right: Victorian colour plate of pointers, the rare type of working dog whose collars the dog collar man did not stock. (Wellcome Library, London)

Right: Dog collar seller from Mayhew's *Life in London*.

41 | Dancing Dogs

Dogs are clever and can be trained to do many different tasks. Dancing is popular today; however, it is far from a new phenomenon.

In his survey of London, Henry Mayhew provided a narrative from a man who had a troop of dogs trained to perform a multitude of tricks. The man was originally from Italy (although the narrative was given in broken French), from where he had brought ten dogs. The description goes into great detail about the names of his dogs, the way they were trained and their appearance. Three of his dogs were called Favourite, Finette and Ozor. Each had a dress, jacket and small hat of varying colours, and the main part of their routines consisted of dancing, jumping over a stick and through a hoop. The man was steadfast in stating that he never beat his dogs in order to teach them tricks; instead their training would take up to six weeks.[104]

Vintage dancing dog. (chippix, Shutterstock)

This man stated that he was 73 years old and often had trouble earning enough money for his board and food; on more than one occasion the dogs had to find their own food in the streets. He shared what he had with his dogs and sometimes the children who knew him and his dogs would find something for the animals to eat.[105]

Entertainment dogs were very popular and they had the potential to become very lucrative. In September 1837 an advertisement for the Theatre Royal in Perth, Scotland announced that Mr John Whyte of the Royal Victoria Theatre would be appearing with this famous dog, 'Dragon the 2nd' for six nights in the metro-drama of *The Dog of Montargis*.[106]

Clown en collerette, se précipita sur le panneau.

A poodle rides on the back
of a horse in the circus ring.
(Mary Evans Picture Library)

Blind street musician Charles
Wood and his dancing dog
Bob, 1816. (Mary Evans
Picture Library

Right: Performing dogs.
(Library of Congress)

COPYRIGHT 1899
COURIER LITHO. CO.
BUFFALO.

42 | Rudyard Kipling

Kipling, born in India in December 1865, is another one of Britain's famous writers whose talents included poetry, history and fiction. Probably his most famous novel was *The Jungle Book*, published in 1894.

Kipling's life was not without hardship. Two of his children died in his lifetime: the first, Josephine, when she was only a young child, and the second, John, during the First World War at the Battle of Loos in September 1915. He later published a history of the Irish Guards, the regiment in which his son had served, as well as many volumes on military subjects such as the training of the new armies during the First World War and the war at sea.

Saying goodbye to a beloved pet. (Everett Collection, Shutterstock)

Kipling wrote of the great sorrow that a dog can bring, when the inevitable time comes to say goodbye. Asking the reader to consider why they put themselves and their hearts through such turmoil.

The Power of a Dog
There is sorrow enough in the natural way
From men and women to fill our day;
But when we are certain of sorrow in store,
Why do we always arrange for more?
Brothers and sisters I bid you beware
Of giving your heart to a dog to tear.

Buy a pup and your money will buy
Love unflinching that cannot lie–
Perfect passion and worship fed
By a kick in the ribs or a pat on the head.
Nevertheless it is hardly fair
To risk your heart for a dog to tear.

When the fourteen years that nature permits
Are closing in asthma or tumors or fits
And the vet's unspoken prescription runs
To lethal chambers, or loaded guns.
Then you will find – its your own affair
But – you've given your heart to a dog to tear.

When the body that lived at your single will
When the whimper of welcome is stilled (how still!)
When the spirit that answered your every mood
Is gone – wherever it goes – for good,
You still discover how much you care
And will give your heart to a dog to tear.

We've sorrow enough in the natural way
When it comes to burying Christian clay.
Our loves are not given, but only lent,
At compound interest of cent per cent.
Though it is not always the case, I believe,
That the longer we've kept 'em the more do we grieve;

For when debts are payable, right or wrong,
A short time loan is as bad as a long–
So why in Heaven (before we are there)
Should we give our hearts to a dog to tear?

Rudyard Kipling. (Library of Congress, LC-DIG-ggbain-03724)

Throughout his life many attempts were made to bestow honours and decorations befitting a man who had made such great contributions to literature. He turned down a knighthood but did accept a Nobel Prize for Literature in 1907.

Kipling died in January 1936, aged 70. His ashes were interred in Poets' Corner in Westminster Abbey.

43 | The Hound of the Baskervilles

Sir Arthur Conan Doyle's most famous character, the detective Sherlock Holmes, first appeared in 1887. His home at 221b Baker Street is known just as well as his archetypal deerstalker cap.

His third detective story was *The Hound of the Baskervilles* in 1902. The story is centred around the death of Sir Charles Baskerville in his Devon home, from an apparent heart attack; Holmes is asked to investigate due to the horrified face of the deceased and the large paw prints nearby, which implies something more sinister. As with any good mystery, a legend forms the heart of the story. In this case, it is a legend that exists outside of the novel of a large black dog that exists in many places around the UK and even further afield. Specifically in Devon, the legend of black dogs relate to a local man selling his soul to the devil, a close situation to the fictional tale of the Baskervilles.

Arthur Conan Doyle at work. (Wellcome Library, London)

Sherlock's brilliance is undeniable. However, it is coupled with a tendency to isolate himself that is often a source of frustration, sentiments often expressed by the long-suffering Watson. Holmes and Watson have been portrayed by many actors in the century since the pair first worked together, and many onscreen adaptations have been made from Conan Doyle's original stories. *The Hound of the Baskervilles* is no different, with at least ten film or TV adaptations.

Left: The stunning cover of a 1902 edition of *The Hound of the Baskervilles*.

Below: An original illustration from the *Strand* magazine.

The Kennel Club

The Kennel Club was founded on 4 April 1873 by S.E. Shirley with the intention of setting a consistent and fair set of rules by which to govern the very popular dog shows that had increased in numbers since the first in 1859.[111]

One of the main activities of the club was to create a stud book in order to show the pedigrees of the show winners, as well as guidance on the rules of dog shows. Royal approval was added when the Prince of Wales (the future King Edward VII) became patron, a tradition all of his successors have continued.

Another important role of The Kennel Club was ensuring that dogs that were exhibited at shows under their rules were registered with the club, to make sure as far as possible that the dog was being shown in the correct class and the person doing so was the owner. Monthly lists of registrations appeared in the *Kennel Gazette* from 1880 onwards. In one edition of the magazine, three English setters were registered under the names 'John the Baptist', 'Joseph in Egypt' and 'Abraham's Wife'. These names were accepted by the club but, after protestations by the clerical members, the owner was asked to change their names and a notice duly appeared in the following issue of the gazette:

Sewallis Shirley, the founder of The Kennel Club. (*Kennel Gazette*)

> The names John the Baptist, Joseph in Egypt and Abraham's Wife, notified in the last issue of the 'Kennel Gazette' as having been registered for three English setters, have been changed to Our Jack, Our Joe and Our Sal.[112]

The success of The Kennel Club is shown by its reproduction around the world including: America, Canada, New Zealand and South Africa.

The Kennel Club today runs the annual Crufts show since it acquired it after the death of Mr Charles Cruft. The show is watched by millions and has brought together the two most important organisations in the dog world.

45 | Companions of the Railway

From the late Victorian period possibly through to the 1950s, it would have been commonplace to see a dog at a station, most probably collecting for a local charity or a railwayman's fund. By the 1920s and 1930s, some of these dogs – who had since passed on – were still found collecting for charity from glass cases. Examples of these can still be found at the National Railway Museum and the Bluebell Railway.

These dogs were famous among visitors to stations in London as well as outlying stations such as Newhaven in East Sussex. Often cared for by a railwayman or the station master, they would go about their work of their own accord, jumping on and off trains arriving at the station, and in their own way encouraging passengers to donate to their cause. Regional papers around the country printed notices and articles of the exploits and demise of these dogs.

Some of these dogs have become famous, such as London Jack who collected at Waterloo Station for the Southern Railway Orphanage and is now still collecting on the Bluebell Railway. There were, however, many other dogs who carried out the same role up and down the country for many years.

A dog called Roy collected at Euston Station in the period 1918–25. It was in 1925 that the *Hull Daily Mail* covered his retirement, stating he had raised a total of £3,101 11s 11d during his seven years' service for the London, Midland & Scottish Railway Benevolent Fund. Roy was said to be of mixed ancestry that included both Newfoundland and Scottish collie. However, of late his leap on to the railway carriages had become very laboured and it was decided that Roy should end his days leisurely in retirement. The newspaper gave a detailed report of Roy's method of collection:

London Jack II collects for L&SWR Servants' Orphanage (Mary Evans Picture Library/ PAUL KEEVIL)

London Jack. (Mary Evans/
Natural History Museum)

Knowing that a train is about to leave, he begins at the tail end, and systematically works his way to the foremost coach. A touch on the leg of any charitably disposed person usually proved sufficient reminder of the box on the dog's back, and, as the coin jingles into the box Roy gives one bark as 'Thank you'.

It was also noted in the article that Roy would be looked after by one of the railway staff and that his position was to be filled by Rags, who was a Smithfield sheepdog.

It was not just London-based dogs that made it into the newspapers. Another dog named Jack, who was based out of Lewes Station in East Sussex, was very well known for his journeys up and down to London. Although it is not specified that he collected for charity, he was certainly well known along the line. However, in 1882, while at Norwood Junction Station, his left foreleg was crushed by a train after he slipped while jumping up to the platform. His leg was swiftly amputated

"RAILWAY JACK" (RECENTLY RUN OVER AND WOUNDED AT NORWOOD STATION)   "REGIMENTAL JACK," AN AFGHAN CAMPAIGNER

TWO ADVENTUROUS DOGS

'Two adventurous dogs': Railway Jack and Regimental Jack. (The History Press)

in order to stop any further damage. However, as is the nature of animals, while unattended he removed the bandages and a secondary haemorrhage set in. After this, Jack was closely watched until he recovered. It was stated in the article that Jack would be continuing his job on the railway, albeit in closer proximity to home, and no longer travelling to Paris and Scotland as he had previously. His last adventure had been to a wedding at Berwick, 'and he arrived gaily bedecked with ribbons in honour of the event'.[113] Eight years later, the *York Herald* reported that Jack had passed away at his master's house after reaching the grand age of 13 and having had the honour of being presented to royalty and celebrities alike.[114]

Portrait of Railway Jack (with his front left leg amputated) and his surgeon Mr R.A. Stock. (Mary Evans Picture Library)

It would therefore seem that over the period from 1880 to at least the 1930s, dogs collecting on trains and railways stations would have been an everyday feature of the rail network, something which would be regarded as out of the ordinary today.

THE RAILWAY DOG "HELP," AND HIS MASTER

Another Sussex-based dog, this time with the charitable name of 'Help', was reported in the *Exeter and Plymouth Gazette* of December 1891 as having passed away. Help had been based at Newhaven in East Sussex and had collected more than £1,000 for the orphans of railway men for the Amalgamated Society of Railway Servants. Help was a Scotch collie and was a familiar feature on the train from Newhaven to London Bridge and also occasionally on the 'steamer to France'. It is reported that he 'wore a silver collar, from which depended a silver tablet, on which the object of his mission was engraved'.[115]

Greyfriars Bobby

In an old churchyard in Edinburgh lies the grave of a loyal friend who stood watch over his master until his dying days. The cemetery, known as Greyfriars Kirkyard, had originally been attached to a Franciscan monastery in medieval times until it was dissolved in 1559. After this, the land was designated as a graveyard when other cemeteries closer to the centre of the city had become full. All of the monuments remaining in the churchyard are listed for their historical importance, some of them grand mausoleums and crypts of famous Scottish families. Yet it is a much more humble occupant that probably draws the most public attention at this cemetery.

In 1856 a gardener named John Gray came to Edinburgh with his family and started working as a night watchman for the local police.[116] To keep him company on his lonely patrols around the streets, he took along his Skye terrier, Bobby, the family pet. This continued for many years and the pair became well known to locals. Sadly, John contracted tuberculosis and died in 1858. He was buried in Greyfriars Kirkyard, and after his burial Bobby continued to visit the churchyard, always staying close to his master's grave, even when people tried to stop him. Local people began to realise what little Bobby was doing and erected a shelter for him to sit under while he carried out his lonely vigil. Local people fed him and a cafe opposite the entrance to the cemetery would provide meals for him at lunchtime; each day Bobby would leave the cemetery at 1 p.m. to go and have his lunch there. Tourists began to hear about the dog and would gather to watch Bobby make his way across the street.

When Bobby died on 14 January 1872, aged 16, he had faithfully kept up his watch since his master's death fourteen years previously. Dogs are unable to be buried in consecrated ground, so Bobby couldn't be laid to rest next to his master,

and instead a place was found close to the entrance to the churchyard. In the 1980s a headstone was erected with the inscription:

Greyfriars Bobby, Died 14 January 1872 aged 16 years – Let his loyalty and devotion be a lesson to us all.

Shorty after Bobby's death, a bronze statue was erected in his honour just outside the churchyard, and was allegedly modelled when Bobby was still alive. The statue was originally a water fountain with a basin for humans and a second lower down for dogs, but it is no longer connected to a water supply due to public health fears in the 1970s. A plaque on the statue reads:

A tribute to the affectionate fidelity of Greyfriars Bobby. In 1858 this faithful dog followed the remains of his master to Greyfriars churchyard and lingered near the spot until his death in 1872. With permission erected by Baroness Bardett-Coutts.

The tribute to Greyfriars Bobby near the churchyard.

47 | The Dog Collar Collection

On first mention to friends and family, discussion of this collection brought laughter to those who thought I referred to the collars of vicars. However, on clarification of the true nature of the collection, interest was certainly piqued.

Housed at Leeds Castle, the dog collar collection is unique in the world as it is the only one of its kind on public display. Being allowed to view some of the items during its recent conservation is something I will never forget and is the reason why it is included here.

The original part of the collection was a donation from Mrs Gertrude Hunt, who gave it to the Leeds Castle Foundation after her husband's death. The original sixty collars donated by Mrs Hunt have since been added to by further donations and purchases to make up a picture spanning over 500 years of history. The collection contains collars from countries across Europe, depicting the changing roles of dogs in our history, from spike-hunting and fighting collars, to those for valued pets, show winners, war dogs and celebrities. The inscriptions on many of these collars not only make further research possible, but also encourage a historian to find out more about both the dogs and their owners.

Not all the collars are on display at all times, but below are some favourites from the catalogue.

One collar that really gives a flavour of the dog and its master is from the mid- to late eighteenth century and the inscriptions reads: 'Stop me not but let me jog for I am S. Oliver's Dog.'

Some collars have links to royalty: one is engraved with '"Countess", Honourable Mrs Campbell of Blythswood from HRH Prince Leopold'. The prince was the youngest son of Queen Victoria and Prince Albert; he died at the age of 30 in 1884.

One silver-plated collar is engraved with the coat of arms of the Company of Watermen and Lightermen on one side. On the other is the inscription:

Presented by the Lightermen of the River Thames to 'Roger' as a token of their warm appreciation of the remarkable sagacity shown by him on the occasion of the sinking of the barge 'Eliza' in Northfleet Hope on September 23rd 1896 in arousing them while all unconscious of danger.

The collection has reopened after its conservation and can be viewed whenever the castle is open.

All the information in this section is reproduced from the catalogue of collars kindly supplied by the Leeds Castle Foundation.

A Red Cross dog collar from a German rescue team. (Wellcome Library, London)

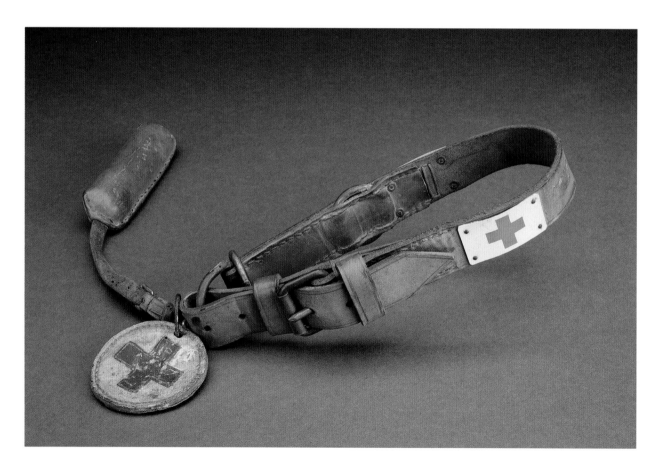

48 | Ratters

When many of us think of dogs that would be good ratters we are inclined to think of terrier breeds, which are small and quick, so best equipped for catching fast rats. We may also associate the role of these dogs with warfare, particularly in the vermin-infested trenches of the Western Front during the First World War. However, long before the war, ratting was a necessity on some of the streets of large cities or rural places. Uncontrolled populations of rats could cause havoc, but hunting them was also a form of entertainment.

Henry Mayhew, who discovered a great deal about the people living in London in the mid-nineteenth century, wrote about a meeting he had with one of the famous organisers of rat-matches, Jimmy (or Jemmy) Shaw. Mayhew seemed rather surprised by the man, stating that 'His statement was certainly one of the most curious that I have listened to, and it was given to me with such a readiness and a courtesy of manner such as I have not often met with during my researches'.[117] Shaw was able to tell Mayhew about his source of rats from country farm workers, warehousemen in the city, sewers and ships. The price he paid for them varied according to the season but was on average 3*d* per rat, and he estimated he would buy 300–700 rats every week for sporting purposes. He entertained some 'first-class chaps' who wanted to test their dogs and also ladies who wished to watch the sport. Shaw was the self-proclaimed oldest and longest-running ratter in the metropolis. He stated that Enfield was the unofficial headquarters for rat-catchers who would not only hunt in their local area but travel all around to find rats that they could sell to Shaw.[118]

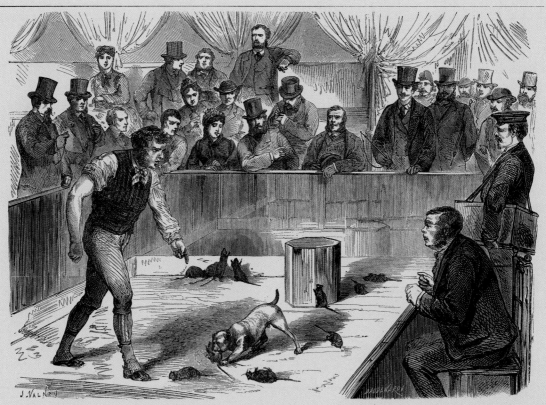

Combat de chiens ratiers et de rats à l'Exposition canine. — Champs-Élysées.

A dog ratting at a dog show in Paris. (Mary Evans Picture Library)

The dog collar collection housed at Leeds Castle in Kent has a dog collar that was presented by Jimmy Shaw himself to a dog, probably on winning a rat-killing contest at his pub.

Some dogs became famous for their ratting talents. One from 1829 was known as Billy and could destroy a quantity of rats in a given time at the Westminster Pit. The newspapers also reported competition for Billy – not a canine rival but a human one. A man named William Hall killed twelve rats with his teeth with his hands tied behind his back. He had exhibited this (as the paper described) 'disgusting' exhibition at a public house in Salford, Manchester.[119]

Ratting was not just for entertainment purposes. With the realisation that rats can carry diseases and destroy produce and stores, catching them became a proper profession; Queen Victoria even had an official rat-catcher. These official rat-catchers were still working in the 1920s as shown in the *Folkestone, Hythe, Sandgate and Cheriton Herald*'s report on the death of Kent County Council's rat-catcher's dog Lady. The report described:

> ... the whippet spaniel bitch which had been his assistant for nine years. This clever animal in its time accounted for many thousands of rodents. During seven weeks, in a certain area on the outskirts of the town, [Dover] it killed a round thousand. 'Lady' met her end in a somewhat tragic manner. The rat catcher had put down some poisoned veal and ham pie by way of bait, and the bitch picked up some of this, with the result that she died almost immediately.[120]

A rat-catcher and his dog walk along a London street. (Mary Evans Picture Library)

When Mr Gosling (the rat-catcher) was interviewed by a reporter from the newspaper, he is quoted as saying in a broken voice that 'I am quite done. Here are a batch of orders I have on hand, including one from Ostend, to clear houses and warehouses of rats, but what can I do?'

49 | Airedale Terrier

The Airedale terrier is, as its name suggests, a member of the terrier class, although it is the largest of that type. He is truly a native of Britain and is thought to have gained its name from the Airedale Show in Yorkshire. The breed's double coat is waterproof, and Airedales make very versatile pets.

The naming of this breed caused some heated discussions, with various suggestions being put into the mix. One name suggested by Hugh Dalziel, who wrote widely on dogs in the late nineteenth century, suggested the Bingley terrier, to illustrate the ancestry of the dog. In his book *British Dogs*, Dalziel showed that he still held on to the idea of calling the dog by this name in the chapter 'The Airedale or Bingley Terrier', where he provided his reasoning for the name. However, the name Airedale terrier became firmly attached to this dog. Despite its 'new' name, it had been a distinct breed in this area of Yorkshire for many decades, where it was used for ratting and otter hunting along the riverbanks. By 1886 The Kennel Club Stud Book had a specific entry for the Airedale terrier.[121]

Airedale. (Lenkadan, Shutterstock)

Their scenting skills are extremely good, which has made them a favourite for police and armed forces around the world. They were the favourite breed of the war dog trainer Edwin Hautonville Richardson, who supplied many for various roles such as messengers, first-aid and guard dogs during the Great War. They were also trained during the Second World War for similar purposes.

The Airedale terrier was a common breed in the early twentieth century. Despite a decline during the middle part of the century it is again becoming popular, even though its original uses in otter hunting and ratting are long past.

50 | Crufts

For those who are not dog breeders or dog owners, Crufts is probably only remembered when the annual event is shown on TV. Although The Kennel Club now runs the Crufts show, they have separate entries in this book, as Crufts is a show whereas The Kennel Club is the authority on breed standards. They also have very different origins.

The first dog show in the UK is agreed to have been at Newcastle in June 1859. It was limited to pointers and setters, had sixty entrants, and had only two prizes up for grabs.[122] After this, many shows were held across the country, including at Birmingham in the same year and later at Leeds and Manchester. Many of these shows were held as additions to yearly agricultural shows and therefore did not stand on their own merit.

Charles Cruft worked as a shop assistant for James Spratt, who produced cakes for dogs, which were hugely popular in the 1860s. Charles Cruft went around as a travelling salesman showing Spratt's dog cakes to dog owners. During this work, he became interested in the breeding and welfare of dogs and believed that well-organised dog shows could achieve both of these aims, enlarging the breeding stock but also showing a large audience how to care for their dogs.[123]

Cruft gained a great deal of knowledge from his attendance at continental dog shows, and in 1886 he held the 'First Great Terrier Show' before managing others. The first show bearing his name, 'Cruft's Great Dog Show', was held in 1891 at the Royal Agricultural

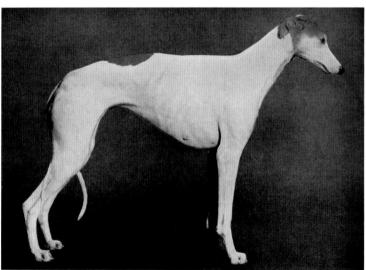

A champion greyhound at Crufts. (The History Press)

EARLY ARRIVALS

IRISH WOLFHOUNDS

RING Nº 1

CHAMPION
TAI YANG OF NEWHAM

JUDGING IN THE RING

A BRUSH UP

SAMOYED ESQUIMAUX SLED

WEST SIBERIAN
SAMOYEDE DOGS

LUNCH TIME

HIS PORTRAIT

S. ROWLES.

Copyrighted in the United States and Canada.

Drawn by S. Rowles.

THE GATHERING OF THE CANINE ARISTOCRACY

With 8033 entries in 1016 classes, Cruft's Dog Show at the Agricultural Hall last week broke all previous world records as regards numbers. Alsatians (713), bulldogs (222), Pomeranians (222), fox-terriers (398), chow-chows (296), Labrador retrievers (412), golden retrievers (229), Scottish terriers (136), and Sealyhams (205) were the most numerous, but all other breeds were well represented, including such larger types as Irish wolfhounds, mastiffs, Borzois, bloodhounds, deerhounds, St. Bernards and Newfoundlands. It is estimated that the value of the dogs was about £150,000, several being priced at over £1000 each. The quality was of a high standard ; no better show, indeed, had been seen.

Hall in Islington.[124] There were around 2,500 entries and 2,000 dogs, and was the first in the world to which all breeds were invited.[125]

After the sinking of HMS *Formidable* on 1 January 1915, Lassie, a dog who had woken a presumed-dead sailor, was exhibited at the show in that year. (This story is discussed later in the book.) In 1917 the annual show stopped due to the First World War and was not rekindled until 1921. It stopped again from 1940 until 1947 due to the Second World War.

Charles Cruft died in September 1938 and his wife took over the running of the 1939 show. After this event The Kennel Club acquired the show. It removed the apostrophe from the title in the 1970s. The number of entries now is over 22,000, a testament to the legacy that Charles Cruft built and the interest he inspired not only in Britain but all over the world.

51 | Police Dogs

The role of bloodhounds as police dogs will be covered in a later section. However, it is important to discuss the wider use of dogs in the police force as well as the breeds used.

A seventeenth-century woodcut of a police dog. A constable goes on his nightly round patrolling the streets. (Mary Evans Picture Library)

Originally police dogs were used to apprehend criminals, or for the protection of the police themselves. When used in this way they were usually Airedale terriers, and were probably provided by Lieutenant Colonel Richardson. It is thought that the first city to have such dogs was Hull, in Yorkshire, in the early twentieth century.[126]

The dogs were taught to recognise anyone in a police uniform as friendly and those without as the enemy. The training was fairly intensive, with the dogs taught to apprehend villains and overcome fear of weapons, and also trained in the agility needed to traverse obstacles in pursuit of a criminal.[127] The use of dogs in the police forces of Britain quickly spread and were soon adopted into forces in Liverpool, Glasgow and Nottingham.

The role of dogs in the police has grown considerably in recent decades. From humble beginnings tracking and detaining criminals, dogs training with the Metropolitan Police now undertake the following:

General purpose: patrolling with their handlers; providing help in searches for people and objects; tracking, chasing and disarming armed suspects.

Detection dogs: for locating drugs, cash, explosives, firearms and human remains.[128]

Today a wide range of breeds are used, such as spaniels for their fantastic ability to pick up scent, German shepherds for their robustness and many other newer breeds to the UK, including Belgian shepherds.

On 22 March 1913 the *Sheffield Evening Telegraph* carried the story 'Famous Dog 'Retires'. The dog, an Airedale terrier, as might be expected during this period, was called Whisk and worked with the police who patrolled the dockside in Hull. The article claimed Whisk was the first dockside police dog and was 7 years old when he retired, having spent six of those years working for the police. The article describes the work Whisk carried out, looking for thieves and tramps concealed in the railway wagons or on timber stacks. It said he had been on duty over 2,000 times in his career and, owing to his eyesight failing, was being withdrawn from service.[129]

Recently, the oldest working police dog, a spaniel named Brewster, retired from his job with the Bedfordshire, Cambridgeshire & Hertfordshire Dog Unit. At 13 years old he had worked for the police for ten years after being donated by owners who could not handle his energetic nature. The police were able to harness his energy and his abilities for use as a detection dog, finding drugs and cash in various parts of the country, and he became one of the unit's most famous dogs. He will now live with his handler and enjoy his retirement, which will include chasing tennis balls and napping.[130]

German Shepherd police dog with his handler. (West Midlands Police)

52 | Protection of Animals

The first animal protection law passed in the United Kingdom was the Cruel Treatment of Cattle Act in 1822, which is sometimes known as Martin's Act. This protected animals such as horses, cows and oxen among others.

Two years later in 1824 the Society for the Protection of Cruelty to Animals was set up and in 1840 it was given its royal prefix. The society was the first of its kind in the world for its care and promotion of animal rights. In 1835 the Cruelty to Animals Act was passed which made baiting of all animals illegal and began to improve the welfare of other animals such as dogs.

In 1849 another step forward was made with the Cruelty to Animals Act 1849, which replaced the previous laws of 1822 and 1835. This act itself was repealed later by the 1911 Protection of Animals Act, which amalgamated amendments and other legislation that had been passed in the interim period.

In 2006, the Animal Welfare Act was passed which again combined previous pieces of legislation into a new Act. In addition, the duty of care of animal owners was introduced, which made it illegal for owners to not provide basic needs such as food and healthcare to their pets. Tail docking was also made illegal if it was carried out for purely cosmetic reasons.

RSPCA Inspector Stamp standing by his vehicle decorated for a dog welfare campaign at a local Branch carnival circa 1930 (RSPCA)

Although this chapter contains no individual dogs, it is important to remember the fight that charities and individuals have made in order to ensure that all animals are looked after and well treated. We should never forget the importance of this legislation in protecting our pets and those who are not afforded the same care that we give our own. There is always more that can be done and that is why charities such as RSPCA, PDSA, Blue Cross, Dog's Trust and many more nationally and locally continue to make us aware of the changes that need to be made in order to safeguard our animals.

53 | Titanic

The whole world was watching when the biggest ship in the world set sail on her maiden voyage on 10 April 1912, heading from Southampton to New York City. She was like a floating palace, exquisitely furnished and luxurious even to those travelling on third-class tickets. Many were travelling to a new life in America, with dreams of a new start on the other side of the Atlantic Ocean.

Opposite: Titanic sinking. (Everett Historical, Shutterstock)

Below: Pets aboard *Titanic* included a pedigree French bulldog. (Aaron Amat, Shuttershock)

When *Titanic* hit an iceberg on the night of 14 April, sinking only hours later in the early morning of 15 April, the press reported on events, survivors and those who perished for weeks afterwards. The sinking was replayed around the world in vivid detail and interviews were given by survivors. However, the story of the dogs travelling on the ship have all but been forgotten.

It is difficult to definitively say how many dogs were on board *Titanic*, as we can only find records for those who are recorded as 'lost' from the reports of passengers and from their claims on their insurance. It is suspected that at least twelve dogs were on board when she sank, either in passengers' cabins or in the ship's kennel situated on F Deck. Each day a member of the crew would walk the dogs around the upper deck of the ship[131] and a dog show had been planned by the first-class passengers to take place on Monday 15 April, had the ship not sunk that very morning.[132]

Some of the dogs have been identified by their owners' later insurance claims and also from survivors' accounts. Many lapdogs are thought to have been present on the ship but, due to their small size, it is impossible to know exactly how many and if they survived. The dogs we know were on board are those of the first-class passengers. John Jacob Astor, the richest man on the ship, had at least one dog on board, his Airedale named Kitty.[133] There was also a pedigree French bulldog named Gamin de Pycombe (belonging to Robert Daniel), a Pekingese named Sun Yat-Sen, at least three Pomeranians, a chow chow, a King Charles spaniel[134] and possibly a Great Dane.

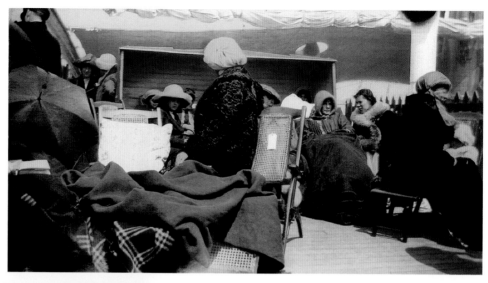

Right: Survivors aboard *Carpathia*. (Everett Historical, Shutterstock)

Below: Beloved pets aboard *Titanic* included at least three Pomeranians like this beautiful example from a vintage photograph. Two were saved – including the pet of Elizabeth Rothschild, who refused to board the rescue ship until they also agreed to take her dog. (Everett Collection, Shutterstock)

Three of the dogs survived. Unsurprisingly these were the smallest ones, which could be easily hidden during embarkation of a lifeboat. Margaret Hay's Pomeranian left the ship in Lifeboat 7 with its owner, and a second Pomeranian, belonging to Elizabeth Rothschild, also survived, in Lifeboat 6. However, *Carpathia*, the ship that rescued them, initially refused to take Rothschild's dog on board, but had to concede whence she refused to go without it.[135] The third Pomeranian, belonging to William Dulles, did not survive the sinking[136] and the final surviving dog was Henry Harper's Pekingese, Sun Yat-Sen, which left in Lifeboat 3.[137]

Some of the first-class owners claimed compensation for the loss of their pets. $750 was awarded to Robert Daniel for the loss of his champion French bulldog.[138]

54 | Assistance Dogs

Dogs have shown their aptitude for many tasks over the centuries, for example by guarding our homes from strangers or saving those floundering in water. Some, such as Lassie the dog from Lyme Regis who had a natural sense for medical problems and identifying minute signs of life (see HMS *Formidable*), did so without any formal training and paved the way for us to refine and expand such wonderful skills. Even today, ways are still being discovered for dogs to discover medical problems and aid us, which is testament to how important it is to study and identify the learning capabilities and skills of all animals. Help from our canine friends is no longer limited to those with visual impairments: those who are deaf, have serious medical conditions or benefit from help to live more independently can be assisted by a dog. Dogs can now help those who suffer from medical conditions such as epilepsy or diabetes to be warned of the start of a seizure or to take medication. They can even be trained to detect cancer in tissue samples.

The beginnings of modern-day assistance dogs can be traced back hundreds of years. Although dogs have been assisting the blind for centuries on an individual basis, the first organised attempts were made in small numbers in Paris in the late 1700s. The outbreak of the First World War, which brought with it a great deal of advancement in medical treatment, also propelled the training of dogs, as they were now required to not only assist those blinded from birth and accident but also by war. The first guide dogs were trained by pioneers in Germany and trials carried out in various locations throughout the 1920s.

The idea was brought to Britain in the 1930s by two women, Muriel Cooke and Rosamund Bond, who had heard about the work done in Switzerland and the US.[139] Today, we accept guide and other assistance dogs as the norm and of great importance to those they help. However, when the movement began, one commentator described how many looked upon it with scepticism, asking how a dog could be trusted with a man's life.[140] Thankfully, the success of early dogs proved their reservations unfounded.

An antique engraving
showing a beggar guided
by a child and a pet
dog. (Wellcome Library,
London)

One Second World War account of the exploits of an early guide dog was told in the 1940s:

> I have called Fly my 'War Dog' and she deserved that description for the manner in which she enabled me to meet the consequences of enemy action. In those blitz days we had our share, and more, of that enemy action, with my place of employment right in the target area-docks ... There were very real difficulties, quite bad enough for sighted people, but almost unsurpassable for a blind person. But Fly did so well that I was able to go through some nine months of regular blitzes, getting to and from my work without the loss of a single hour.[141]

Today many of the charities that provide assistance dogs have breeding centres for the purposes of breeding dogs particularly suited for the roles required. For example, Guide Dogs for the Blind have a dedicated breeding centre which will allow them to breed up to 1,500 puppies a year for their work.[142]

"WHEN NIGHT SETS IN THE SUN IS DOWN."
From the painting by R. Caton Woodville.

A First World War postcard of Caton-Woodville's painting 'When Night Sets In the Sun is Down'. Soldiers like this became some of the first to use specially trained guide dogs. (Wellcome Library, London)

A guide dog wearing his working backpack and handle. (Treasure dragon, Shutterstock)

55 | Bloodhounds

Bloodhounds have been used for centuries for tracking. In medieval times they would have searched for wounded quarry, and in more recent years it has been humans. The role of the bloodhound as a tracking dog is due to its persistence, ignoring any other scent that could easily distract other dogs. Many other breeds such as collies, lurchers and Airedales are suitable for use as tracking dogs, and our police forces use many breeds to locate humans, drugs, explosives and even money. However, bloodhounds have historically held the role of criminal tracking.[143]

Edwin Hautonville Richardson was a British dog trainer who travelled the world providing dogs to the police and military as well as private individuals. He worked with bloodhounds in Britain, training them to find people hidden in remote places. This training paid off when his dogs were called on to assist in over 4,000 police incidents, to find missing people, murderers and thieves.[144]

One such incident involved a grandmother who had gone missing from her family home on the east coast of Scotland. It was thought that she had gone to Glasgow on the train, but there had been no sighting of her in the city. Richardson was asked to take his hounds to the home and look for her. By the time he arrived it had been two days since her disappearance. The hounds, one of which was Richardson's successful tracker Solferino (or Solly for short) decided against the route to the railway station and instead started in the opposite direction, up a hill and into a wood. Clues were found on the way such as a piece of material belonging to the woman's clothing while the hounds continued on the scent. Unfortunately, the grandmother was not found alive, but the dogs had proven their usefulness in tracking a scent.[145]

Richardson did most of his writing and work with bloodhounds before the First World War. He stated afterwards that the war made it difficult for anyone to keep large dogs such as bloodhounds well fed and cared for. This resulted in the breed diminishing in Britain and it was available only to the wealthy, far beyond the finances of the police at the time: a pure-bred and well-trained adult bloodhound

after the war could have cost anywhere between £50–£200.[146] It was not just the cost of bloodhounds which made them unfeasible, but also the increase in the use of tarmac. Before the installation of proper roads, bloodhounds had been able to track extremely well along roads, paths and fields. However, tar was a substantial obstacle as it does not retain scent as well, and the increasing number of cars meant a criminal could escape quicker than ever before, often before a dog could even be brought to the scene.[147]

Bloodhounds are instantly recognisable by their saggy faces and sad eyes. Their loyalty and perseverance are well known, as is their companionship, as told in a poem written by Bryan Waller Procter under the pseudonym of Barry Cornwall:

Come, Herod, my hound, from the stranger's floor!
Old friend – we must wander the world once more!
For no one now liveth to welcome us back:
So, come! let us speed on our fated track.
What matter the region – what matter the weather,
So you and I travel, till death, together?

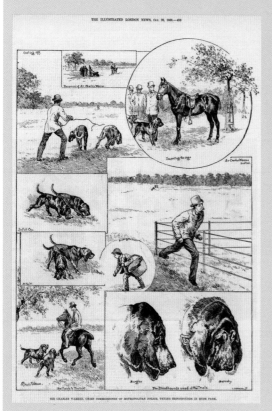

And in death? – why e'en there I may still be found
By the side of my beautiful, black bloodhound ...

What, Herod, old hound! dost remember the day
When I fronted the wolves like a stag at bay?
When downwards they galloped to where we stood,
Whilst I staggered from dread in the dark pine wood?
Dost remember their howlings? their horrible speed?
God, God! how I prayed for a friend in need!
And – he came. Ah! 'twas then, my dear Herod, I found
That the best of all friends was my bold bloodhound.

Men tell us, dear friend, that the noble hound
Must for ever be lost in the worthless ground;
Yet, 'Courage' – 'Fidelity' – 'Love' – (they say)
Bear man, as on wings, to his skies away.
Well, Herod – go tell them whatever may be,
I'll hope I may ever be found by thee.
If in sleep – in sleep: if with skies around
May'st thou follow e'en thither, my dear bloodhound.[148]

56 | Caesar

Edward VII (1901–10) was the eldest son of Queen Victoria and Prince Albert, born in 1841. He was until recently also the longest-serving heir apparent – not surprising considering the length of his mother's reign! Prince Charles, son of Queen Elizabeth II, has recently surpassed Edward, just as Elizabeth has recently overtaken Queen Victoria as the longest-reigning monarch.

H.M. KING EDWARD VII. AND "CAESAR"

COPYRIGHT.   POTTLE. WIMBORNE

Edward VII's was a relatively short reign compared to that of his mother and other monarchs of the twentieth century. He was nearly 60 when he ascended to the throne and, towards the end of his reign, he suffered with a type of skin cancer, bronchitis and other medical issues. He died during a period of constitutional upheaval, which after his death led to legislation that ended the ability of the House of Lords to veto bills passed from the House of Commons.

King Edward had inherited his parents' love of animals, he was very fond of one dog in particular: Caesar.

Caesar was a wire-coated terrier born in 1898. King Edward became greatly attached to this little dog, who was given to him in 1902 after his previous dog had died suddenly after choking on food. What makes Caesar's story different to other royal animals is the importance that was afforded him after the death of his master. It is undeniable that Edward prized Caesar, but this was also reflected in the funeral procession, when Caesar walked behind his master's coffin in front of all the other heads of state, including Kaiser Wilhelm II, who it is said was greatly insulted.

FRANKLYN'S CIGARETTES.

FUNERAL OF EDWARD VII.

After King Edward's funeral a book was published called *Where's Master?* This was a first-person perspective from Caesar himself between the time of Edward VII's death and funeral. It proved to be very popular, and even the toy company Steiff produced toys based on the dog in the early twentieth century.

Caesar died on 18 April 1914 under anaesthetic for an operation. He had been ill and the operation was attempted as a last resort to help him. The report recalls how Caesar had refused to eat after the king's death and became Queen Alexandra's 'constant companion at Marlborough House'.[149]

On Caesar's death in 1914 *The Times* published a piece about him, which covered his life with King Edward and afterwards. Caesar had travelled widely with the king and wore a medal on his collar that identified him as the king's dog.[150] A memorial was raised to Caesar at Marlborough House, which read:

> Our Beloved Caesar who was the King's faithful and constant companion until death and my greatest comforter in my loneliness and sorrow for four years after. Died April 18th 1914.

A car mascot of Caesar went on sale at Bonhams in 2009. It had reportedly been used on various royal cars during King Edward's reign. The mascot sold for just over £4,000.[151]

Edward VII in tweed plus-fours with his dog. (Mary Evans Picture Library)

57 | The Brown Dog

In February 1903 a typical event took place in the teaching rooms of University College London in front of students. A live brown dog laid on a table was operated upon in order to find out how certain procedures would affect it. This process was called vivisection and was completely legal at this time. Many teaching institutions, though not all, used the method in order to advance scientific knowledge and it undoubtedly contributed to medical understanding. Opinions on vivisection had been growing more negative over the years and Queen Victoria was opposed to it – unsurprisingly as she was a dog enthusiast.

On this particular day, two female students who had enrolled at the London School of Medicine for Women and were anti-vivisectionists had come to the university with the purpose of recording such acts. Leisa Schartau and Louise Lind af Hageby were from Sweden and had formed the Anti-Vivisection Society of Sweden. After witnessing numerous vivisections they presented a diary that they had kept to Stephen Coleridge, the secretary of the National Anti-Vivisection Society, which had been set up in 1875.

The account of the vivisection of the brown dog particularly worried Coleridge as, judging from what the two women had written, he suspected that the procedures and rules that were in place to protect the animals were not being observed. He worried that the surgeon, Dr William Bayliss, was not anaesthetising the dog properly and prolonging the suffering of the creature. At that time a case involving vivisection against a surgeon could only be brought with the permission of the Home Secretary. Unfortunately, the current incumbent of this position was not sympathetic to the opinions of the anti-vivisectionists. Therefore Coleridge decided instead to speak out against the procedure and the doctor publically.

Following Coleridge's public discussion of the incident, William Bayliss filed a lawsuit against Coleridge for libel. The case was tried at the Old Bailey in November 1903 and, after days of testimony, William Bayliss won. His damages

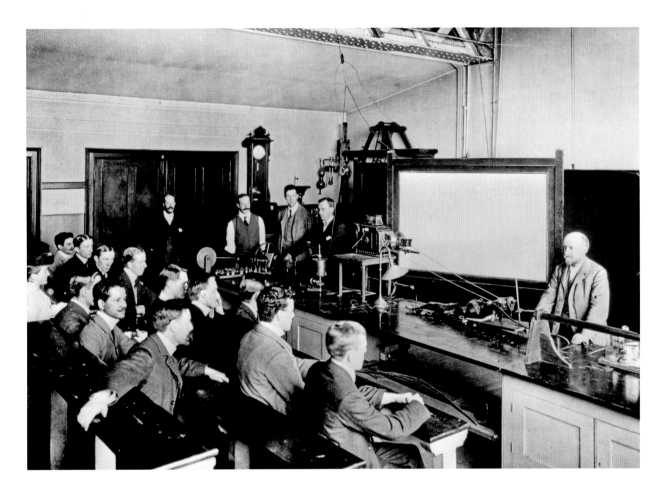

The experiment which led to the Brown Dog case. Behind the table, from left to right, are: unknown; H.H. Dale; E.H. Starling; W.M. Bayliss; unknown. (Wellcome Library, London)

and legal fees were ordered to be paid by Coleridge, who was helped by a London tabloid that launched a fund in order to raise the money.

Although the case had been lost, the work of the anti-vivisectionists was publically aired and received a lot of celebrity support. A statue was designed to memorialise the dog and was erected in Battersea at the Latchmere Recreation Ground in 1906. After the erection of the statue, a series of riots began to occur, organised by medical and veterinary students, over the issue and particularly over the inscription on the statue:

In memory of the Brown Terrier Dog Done to Death in the Laboratories of University College in February 1903 after having endured Vivisections extending over more than two months and having been handed over from one Vivisector to another till death came to his Release.

Also in the memory of the 232 dogs vivisected in the same place during the years 1902–3.

Men and Women of England

How Long shall these things be?

The statue became the focal point for these riots and required seven police officers a day to protect it. After so much controversy, the matter was discussed by Parliament and it was eventually decided by the local council that the statue would be removed. This happened on the night of 10 March 1910 so as not to arouse opposition. It is believed that the statue was destroyed and then melted down.

In 1985 a new memorial to the brown dog was erected in Battersea Park. Vivisection is no longer the main reason for which the dog stands, and it instead stands for the divisive situation of animal testing which still happens in laboratories all over the world. It certainly serves as a reminder to the past and to another role that dogs have undertaken, although unwillingly, in human history.

58 | Rover

Rin Tin Tin and Lassie have been childhood favourites all around the world for decades. They were the heroes of screen and television, portraying the loyalty, faithfulness and intelligence that everybody wanted in a childhood companion. Their names are synonymous with foiling the bad guys and rescuing the wounded.

However, years before them, a British canine was the star of the silver screen in a short six-minute film in 1904. It was a production by Cecil Hepworth, who would become a master of film, and this work, despite its crudeness and overacting as we would judge it today, was actually pioneering for its time due to its narrative coherence.[152] The film was to make history in many ways, the central role of the dog being only one of these. Nowadays we expect to see a story unfold on the screen, where characters come and go, plots are developed and the story continues until it reaches an end. However, film in the early twentieth century was very different.

The six-minute film was called *Rescued by Rover* and it was a family production with all but two members of the cast being related. Cecil Hepworth's wife had written the story and also starred as the mother; Cecil played the father; his baby Barbara was the rescuee; and Blair the family dog played Rover.

The film began with a scene where Rover and the baby are together in the family living room. After this scene, the nurse is shown taking the child out in the pram for a walk in the park, where she refuses to give money to a beggar woman. While the nurse is distracted talking to a soldier, the beggar woman takes the child and leaves, taking the child back to her lodgings. When the nurse returns and tells the tale of the missing child to the mother she is distraught, but Rover, upon hearing and seeing the distress of his mistress, leaps out of the window and begins his search for the missing member of his family. The film then follows Rover as he runs down the street, swims across the river and opens doors in his search. He finally locates the baby, but is pushed away by the beggar woman. We then follow Rover as he runs home to find his master, where he appeals to him to follow him.

Dog and master then take the same route to the location of the beggar woman together. Upon finding her, the baby is saved and Rover is the hero.

This film was popular, much to the surprise of Cecil Hepworth. He had to remake the film three times in order to satisfy demand because the negatives were worn out through making 400 copies of it.[153]

Rover was a rough-coated collie. He continued his acting career in another film called *The Dog Outwits the Kidnapper* in 1908, where he again rescued little Barbara Hepworth from a kidnapper. Rover follows the kidnapper as he steals the child and drives away in a car. The car finally stops after travelling a distance and the kidnapper gets out and enters a house, leaving enough time for Rover to climb into the car and drive it away and return home. The driving scene is very cleverly done, with the dog seemingly driving the vehicle and concentrating. The final scenes of the film show Rover and his ward sitting in the car, with Rover pawing at the steering wheel and looking very pleased with himself.

In his memoirs, Cecil Hepworth recalled Blair's death and recounted a fond memory of him:

A scene from *The Dog Outwits the Kidnapper*, 1908.

... he was a true friend and a great companion, but my most persistent memory of him is the way every morning in life he jumped on a washing basket by my dressing table and waited and longed for a dab on the nose from my shaving brush. Then, with every expression of ineffable happiness, he licked off every trace of soap and waited for more.[154]

So, today when you see dogs used in films, think back to Rover and the path he paved for them.

59 | Nana

J.M. Barrie, the author of *Peter Pan*, may never have imagined how famous his play would become when it was first performed in 1904. Numerous animated and film adaptations have reinvented it, making it a timeless tale that both adults and children can relate to.

James Barrie. (Library of Congress, LC-USZ62-89798)

In Barrie's original, the play begins in the hub of the Darling home, and we are introduced to the nursery and the ever-faithful Nana. At the strike of the clock she jumps into action, readying the nursery before leaving and re-entering with Michael on her back, who is complaining about having a bath.

Barrie gave careful guidance in specifying Nana's demeanour and how her role should be acted by a human. The rest of the characters come from real-life adventures lived out in summer holidays taken with Barrie's friends and their children so it is therefore only to be expected that Nana herself has a real dog at her core. In reality, Nana is not inspired by one dog but two.

Mary and James Barrie had two pet dogs during their marriage. Porthos was the first, a St Bernard who was purchased by Barrie for his new wife in Lucerne, Switzerland, while on their honeymoon.[155] Although he officially belonged to Mary, it was James who won the dog's affections, and Porthos was part of the many adventures with the Lost Boys.

After seven years, Porthos passed away and it was a few years before the Barries took on another dog, this time a black-and-white Newfoundland named Luath.[156] It is presumed that Nana's coat is a direct connection to Luath, as her described coat and colourings match Luath's. However, underneath the Newfoundland coat, it is supposedly Porthos the St Bernard who inspired Nana's character.[157]

Nana is a lovable character and portrays the role that so many dogs play in our lives – of friendship, loyalty and, of course, as protector of our families in our childhood games and reality – whether we choose to grow up or not!

Michael rides on the back of the dog Nana. Illustration by Alice B. Woodward in *The Peter Pan Picture Book*, 1907. (Mary Evans Picture Library)

60 | War Dog School

Before the outbreak of the First World War, some trainers and breeders of dogs around the world could see the potential in using dogs for military purposes such as finding the wounded on the battlefield, sending messages and pulling guns and supplies. Many nations such as France, Germany, Austria-Hungary and Russia trialled dogs within their military and police forces successfully and then continued to train and use dogs during the war. However, although in Britain dogs were used by many police services across the country, the military had steadfastly rejected the idea.

It took until July 1917 for a war dog school to be set up on the artillery ranges near Shoeburyness, Essex. Once opened, Edwin Hautonville Richardson, a world-renowned trainer who had been petitioning the War Office for years about the benefits of training dogs, got to work. He trained dogs to carry messages, guard depots and ammunition stores both at home and abroad, and to act as sentries.

It wasn't until 1918 that these dogs reached the Western Front in any great number, but once there they provided assistance to infantry units in the front lines by sending messages back to battalion and brigade headquarters about objectives and situations during both small- and large-scale offensives. When human message runners were killed, wounded or got lost in the mud and devastation of the battle-fields, it was the dogs of the British Messenger Dog Service who provided a faster and more fleeting target for the enemy.

Stories of some of these dogs' efforts during the war can be found in Richardson's memoirs and a notable one is about a dog named Tweed who had done fantastic work, as the report says, with his unit near Amiens. Tweed was a grey Old English Sheepdog, although the breed has changed remarkably in the past 100 years. A report of his work was sent back by his handler Private Reid of the Royal Canadian Hussars:

On May 2nd 1918, I was sent to the 18th Div[ision]. There were no dogs that had been up before. On May 2nd at 10 p.m. the Hun came over on the Q.V.R. [Queen's Victoria Rifles] – my dog was up at their Batt[alion] Hdqtrs. They were cut off from the London Reg[iment]; they released 'Tweed' with the message 'Send reinforcements and small round ammunition.' He came through a Boche barrage – three kilo[metres] in 10 mins ... On May 8th I was with the Australians 48th Batt[alion]. They had moved forward, no runner could cross the open in the daytime – pigeons could not fly at night, they were in a bad place, so they sent for 'Tweed'. He made three runs at night, and one of the runs he was out on patrol; they sent him back with a message 'The Germans are preparing for a raid' and spoiled the Hun's plans.[158]

Dog-handler reading a message brought by a messenger dog, in France, during the First World War. (National Library of Scotland)

Tweed had almost been rejected as a messenger dog as he didn't initially show the right qualities for the service due to his sensitive nature. However, Mrs Richardson protested at him being discarded, and more effort was put into his handling. It wasn't always messages of importance for offensive action that Tweed was responsible for, but also those for other requirements, such as 'send socks'.

Richardson's own description of Tweed does him real credit: 'His demeanour in war always seemed to me to be to be typically British, carrying as it did a quiet dignity and with no desire to quarrel, but at the same time when he did get going there was no doubt as to the certainty of his methods.'[159]

These dogs weren't always readily accepted by the units to whom they were attached, and many officers doubted how useful they could really be. In *The Daily Telegraph* in 1918, writing about his experiences during the war and the struggle he had to gain recognition for his work, Richardson said:

... the long uphill struggle, the open sneers, the active obstructions, the grudging assistance, all was forgotten in the knowledge that countless men's lives had been saved and that this fact had now been realised and acknowledged.[160]

61 | Blue Cross in the First World War

Many charities helped wounded animals on the front lines by fundraising or providing medical aid, both at home and abroad, during the First World War. Charities also funded dog licences for masters who were fighting abroad and covered the quarantine costs of those who otherwise could not have afforded to bring their beloved pets home from the front. Blue Cross and RSPCA are just two of the many charities who aided man and dog during the conflict. Here it is pertinent to give further information about how Blue Cross fundraised for the care of dogs and horses amongst other animals and also some of the wonderful, heart-warming stories that they made possible.

The Blue Cross Fund was set up by the Our Dumb Friends' League in 1912. During the First World War this fund was used to care for animals in conflicted areas of the Western Front. In France they cared for thousands of horses used by the Allied armies as well as the dogs that were used. The French War Office handed over the care of all of their war dogs to Blue Cross.[161]

Blue Cross had to raise money in order to carry out this necessary role, and one way they did this was to sell books of poetry written about the animals, mainly horses but also dogs. In 1917 Blue Cross created *A Book of Poems for the Blue Cross Fund (To Help Horses in War Time)*, which was reprinted twice that same year. Fifty-nine poems fill the pages on various subjects, such as the comradeship between horses or dogs and humans, wounded animals and appeals for help on behalf of those who cannot ask for themselves.

One poem that appears in the book is entitled 'Scottie'

One paw uplifted as if in surprise,
Shaggy hair sheltering bonnie brown eyes –
Only a doggie – but looking so wise!
That's Scottie.

Are you downhearted, or sad, or morose?
Scottie would willingly banish your woes –
Into your hand slides a little cold nose!
That's Scottie.

Or are you merry and happy and gay?
Some one is equally ready for play,
Scampering madly and doubling the way!
That's Scottie.

Dear loving heart in your little rough coat,
Turning your mood to our every note,
Loyally blind to our every mote!
That's Scottie.

Faithfullest friend that a man ever had,
Sticking the closer if Fortune be bad –
No one need ever feel lonely or sad
With Scottie![162]

An original Blue Cross poster for the Our Dumb Friends' League, raising money for horses at the Western Front. (Library of Congress, LC-USZC4-11251)

Opposite: 'Wild with joy': pets greeting their owner, on leave from the trenches. (The History Press)

At the end of the war, when many servicemen wanted to bring home the canine friends they had made, Blue Cross stepped in again by establishing kennels for the six-month quarantine that was necessary. Special kennels in Charlton were taken over for this purpose, and by 1920 351 dogs had been cared there since the armistice.

Some of the heartfelt messages that Blue Cross received from happy owners after their pets had returned from quarantine are testament to the fantastic work and effort that the charity, along with others, put into caring for and paying for the pets of servicemen during and after the war.

One such message from Liverpool says it all:

You will be pleased to know that 'Basil' arrived at 7pm and that he was in beautiful condition after his long journey … I approached the hamper containing 'Basil' without speaking and in a few seconds he had scented me. He barked, and howled, and made such a noise that soon a little crowd of spectators gathered … I just managed to open one corner and 'Basil' scrambled out and jumped on to my shoulder, barking and licking my hands and face. It was a revelation to me, and I shall never forget 'Basil's' greeting. After giving him a drink of water, I took him home in a taxi, and he soon settled down in his new surroundings.

Old times, places and adventures came flooding back to me as I watched 'Basil,' and my heart is full of gratitude to you, and The Blue Cross Fund, for all the kindness shown to me and 'Basil.'

Through the help of The Blue Cross Fund, I have had restored to me a faithful companion, 'Basil,' who shared with me the few pleasures and comforts, also the perils and hardships of a soldier's life, during the great war. Please accept the heartfelt thanks from a lover of all animals and birds.[163]

62 | Prince

There are countless stories of the heroism of both humans and animals during the First World War. These tales of selflessness and great kindness happened during a conflict that entangled the world and changed it forever. One of the most touching is not a tale of bravery in battle or sacrifice for another, but one that shows the resilience of the bond between a man and his dog, across the sea and through a foreign land.

"THE WANDERER SPRANG TOWARDS HIS MASTER WITH DELIGHT"

Prince was an Irish terrier whose master served as a regular soldier with the North Staffordshire Regiment. Private Brown left his wife and Prince behind in Ireland (where the battalion had been based) when he went to France in September 1914. His wife visited her husband's parents in Stafford, England, shortly thereafter and from there went back home to Hammersmith. Prince had been inconsolable since his master left and eventually disappeared from his London home. Mrs Brown wrote to her husband telling him of Prince's disappearance. When she received a letter from her husband, the contents was almost unbelievable; Prince was safe with him in France.

Prince had taken it upon himself to track down his master across England, the Channel and through France. He was brought home after the war and lived with his master until 1921 when he sadly died after eating some poisoned meat.

Dog and owner reunited in the trenches in France. Here the artist has made a mistake in depicting Prince, as Irish terriers have red coats. (Mary Evans Picture Library)

63 | Edith Cavell (1865–1915)

The story of Nurse Edith Cavell is one that many people are familiar with from the First World War, especially as 2015 was the centenary of her execution. Her defiance of the German authorities, even after being sentenced to death, still stands as a testament to her courage and willingness to help the wounded, regardless of their nationality. Cavell was guilty of not only treating wounded Allied soldiers (British, French and Belgian) but also of aiding their escape into neutral Holland and, as the German authorities saw it, helping those men to return to their respective armies to possibly fight against the Germans. Edith Cavell was executed by firing squad in October 1915 in Belgium, along with several other conspirators.

Edith Cavell was born near Norwich, the daughter of a reverend. She trained as a nurse at The London Hospital in Whitechapel under Matron Eva Luckes (who has recently become a well-known figure since the *Casualty 1900s* TV series), who had been a friend of Florence Nightingale. Cavell was extremely successful in her chosen profession, becoming a pioneer of modern nursing in Belgium, and by the outbreak of war she was working with many hospitals and schools teaching nursing. When the First World War broke out she was visiting her mother in Norwich, but she returned to Brussels to her clinic, which was being used by the Red Cross.

Brussels was under German occupation from late August 1914, and at her clinic, Cavell began sheltering wounded and trapped British, Belgian and French soldiers as well as Belgian civilians of military age. Cavell formed only part of a circle of people who helped these men to gain false papers and escape to neutral Holland; her actions were in direct violation of German military law. She was betrayed and on 3 August 1915 she was arrested. There has been a lot of debate surrounding the legality of her execution and over which offense she was ultimately charged with. Nonetheless she was executed on 12 October 1915.

In Allied propaganda she was presented as a heroine. This helped fuel the idea of the 'beastly Hun' who (along with other atrocities, such as the burning of the

Edith Cavell with her dogs Jack and Don. (Wellcome Library, London)

Belgian village Louvain) had killed Edith Cavell, an English rose.

Before the start of the First World War, Edith was pictured in Belgium with her two dogs. After her execution, a notebook was found with her belongings at the hospital she worked in, in which she had written about the care of dogs. The original pages are held by the Imperial War Museum, but much of the information and also her drawings were published in 1934 in association with The National Canine Defence League (now Dog's Trust) along with a biographical introduction by Rowland Johns, a well-known dog author of the period.

Johns tells the story of Cavell's early life, nursing and capture. Even in the lead up to her trial and subsequent execution, Cavell enquired about her beloved dog, Jack, and asked the sister of the hospital to brush him every day.[164] Cavell's notebook describes how to care for dogs, and included ideas on kennels, bedding, food, water, exercise and grooming, as well as a lengthy piece on the watchdog. Charming drawings by Cavell also accompany the sections relating to kennels.

It appears that Edith Cavell had two dogs, Don and Jack. Don is believed to have passed away a few years before the war, but Jack outlived his mistress by many years. Jack's life was fairly turbulent after her death, as those who worked in the hospital said he would howl after his mistress and was clearly missing her. His temperament was not very good during this time and he would sometimes bite nurses and other staff. After many changes in ownership and various new kennels, he finally found a home with the Dowager Duchess de Croÿ, whose family had taken part in hiding fugitives alongside Edith Cavell. There Jack lived for another seven years and enjoyed life with the other dogs. He is described as being of no breed, the size of a small shepherd's dog with grey hair on his back, a lighter coloured chest and fawn legs.[165] He was preserved after his death and is currently looked after by the Imperial War Museum.

64 | HMS Formidable

HMS *Formidable* was a pre-dreadnought battleship, built in 1898 and commissioned in 1904. When war broke out in 1914 she was assigned to the English Channel Fleet to guard the coast in case of a German invasion. She was torpedoed in the early hours of New Year's Day 1915 and although it was hoped she could make it to shore, she began to list sharply and was struck by a second torpedo.

Captain Loxley of the Royal Navy, his terrier Bruce by his side, gives a warning of torpedoes to another ship. (©Illustrated London News Ltd/Mary Evans Picture Library)

The crew was evacuated in tough conditions and the weather was only getting worse. As the ship sank, Captain Loxley oversaw the evacuation from the ship's bridge with his fox terrier, Bruce, by his side. One survivor's report that was printed in *The Times* said, 'The captain's old terrier Bruce was standing on duty at his side on the fore-bridge to the last.'[166] The bad sea and weather made evacuation difficult and many of the lifeboats were launched upside down. In all, over 500 men were lost. The body of Captain Loxley's loyal dog was washed up in Dorset after the sinking and was buried in a named grave in Abbotsbury Subtropical Gardens.

One of HMS *Formidable's* lifeboats was blown along the coast to Lyme Regis where the survivors were reportedly given a stiff drink and cigarettes. The bodies of seven men from the lifeboat who had died were taken to the local pub, the Pilot Boat, and placed in the cellar as a makeshift mortuary.

The wife of the landlord of the pub suffered from epileptic episodes and they had a cross-bred collie who would

Captain Loxley and his dog Bruce of HMS *Formidable*. (©Illustrated London News Ltd/Mary Evans Picture Library)

Front cover of *The Sketch* magazine, January 1915, showing Bruce. (©Illustrated London News Ltd/Mary Evans Picture Library)

wake her after an attack by licking her face. The dog managed to get into the cellar where the bodies had been laid and began licking the face of one of the sailors. She continued to do this for around thirty minutes, trying to rouse him and keep him warm. Amazingly, this sailor, Able Seaman John Cowan began to stir, whereupon he was promptly removed from the cellar.

In the list of survivors printed in *The Times* on 2 January, Cowan's name is not listed, possibly because those who were taken to the Pilot Boat had not yet been officially recorded with the authorities. He does, however, appear on the list in the issue of 4 January.

Cowan returned to be photographed with his saviour, whose name was Lassie. It has been suggested by locals and other historians that this dog was actually the inspiration for Eric Knight's *Lassie*; however, there is no evidence to prove this.

A HEROINE OF THE WAR AT CRUFT'S.

Lassie, the hero of HMS *Formidable*. (©Illustrated London News Ltd/Mary Evans Picture Library)

H.M.S. FORMIDABLE.

SYMONDS & CO. PORTSMOUTH.

429 G. BEAGLES POSTCARDS

THIS ILL-FATED BATTLESHIP SANK IN THE ENGLISH CHANNEL AFTER A TERRIBLE EXPLOSION IN THE EARLY MORNING OF 1st JANUARY, 1915. A TERRIBLE GALE WAS RAGING, AND ONLY 199 OF OUR BRAVE SAILORS WERE SAVED OUT OF ABOUT 750. THE GALLANT CAPTAIN BEING AMONGST THE DROWNED.

A vintage postcard of the HMS *Formidable*, with a portrait of Captain Loxley. (The History Press)

65 | Regimental Mascots

Animals have a long, dynamic history with the armed forces of our nation, playing a very important role both at home and during operations that is often underestimated. While the animals themselves vary throughout history, from lions, monkeys, goats, sheep, ponies, rabbits, cats and, probably most commonly, dogs, their lives and the lives of servicemen are thoroughly intertwined.

Sammy, the mascot of the Northumberland Fusiliers regiment. (©Illustrated London News Ltd/Mary Evans Picture Library)

The First World War had a large civilian volunteer and conscript army, which brought with it many mascots and friends which shared the troubles and hardships of life during the war. Some of these mascots came from home, bringing reminders of what servicemen would return to after the conflict, and others were strays, displaced just like the human population of France and Belgium, looking for a new home, food and comfort.

There are thousands of stories that would aptly illustrate this point. One of these is of Sammy, a Border terrier and mascot of the 4th Northumberland Fusiliers, who accompanied his comrades during their training and also when they were sent abroad to the Western Front in spring 1915. One officer wrote of the departure from home, describing the send off from other officers, men and civilians at the local railway station. He goes on to list the officers who travelled on the train, finishing with 'as well as "Sammy", our regimental pet, who would have been miserable if he had been left behind'.[167]

The battalion took part in the Second Battle of Ypres (22 April–25 May 1915); the first day of this battle is most notoriously known for the first use of gas during the conflict. The men of the 4th Northumberland Fusiliers, with Sammy by their side, suffered from the effects of gas during the opening days of the battle. Sammy survived until the autumn of 1916 when he was killed during firing practice.

Sammy was returned home, and the men of the battalion paid for the services of a taxidermist so that Sammy could remain with them once they too returned home. Sammy now resides at Alnwick Castle, the home of the Northumberland Fusiliers Museum. The inscription which accompanies him reads:

'Sammy'
Regimental Pet of the 4th Battalion Northumberland Fusiliers
Landed in France with the battalion on April 20th 1915.
Took part in the attack on St Julien during 2nd Battle
of Ypres, April 26th 1915, and was wounded and gassed in
the subsequent fighting; was with the battalion continuously
until accidently killed during field firing practice at
Warfusee in the Autumn of 1916.

Drummer recovering at the Officer's Hospital, Wynberg, Nr Cape Town. (By kind permission of the Trustees of the Fusiliers Museum of Northumberland)

Mascots and pets had been part of the armed forces long before the First World War, and the Northumberland Fusiliers were no exception. The story of one mascot and his ancestry with the regiment was lovingly conveyed through the *St George's Gazette*, the regimental magazine. A 5-month-old dog named Hettie was a gift to Captain and Brevet-Major G.L.S. Ray and so joined the 5th Battalion at Dover in October 1891. After eighteen months' service her son Drummer was born, the last of a litter of five born at 5 a.m. on 5 February 1893 at Milton, Sittingbourne, Kent.

Just like his mother, Drummer joined the 5th Battalion aged 5 months on 5 July of the same year. Among his adventures, he accompanied the regiment to Aldershot, Portsmouth, Gibralter, Egypt, Crete and home again between 1893 and 1899. Drummer then journeyed with the 1st Battalion to South Africa where, during the conflict, his master was killed. It was stated that Queen Victoria planned to honour Drummer with a medal of his own; the War Office put a stop to that. Drummer did, however, wear miniature versions of the following: Queen's and Egyptian medals with clasps for 'Khartoum'; and South African medal with clasps for 'Belmont', 'Modder River', 'Relief of Kimberley', 'Paardeberg', 'Driefontein', 'Johannesberg' and 'Diamond Hill'. He was also wounded in the shoulder during the South African war and hospitalised with the other wounded officers. It is said that during his active service he would snap at passing bullets like they were flies.

Drummer's end came when he was at Colchester and ate a bone laced with poison, which was meant for the rats, on 20 January 1902.

66 | Nipper

Although you may not know Nipper by name, you will undoubtedly know him from his picture. Nipper's image has been used for over 100 years in advertising for various companies; most familiar to Brits is probably the logo for the store 'His Master's Voice' (or HMV). Although the image has been stylised over the years and is currently a vibrant shade of pink, the picture of Nipper is instantly recognisable. The story of the dog and the painting that made him famous is, however, less well known.

Nipper was born in 1884 and raised by Mark Barraud who worked in stage design. He was thought to be a mixed-breed dog, was predominately white and was named for his delectation in nipping people's legs. Barraud died in 1887 and Nipper went to live with his master's brother, Francis. Francis also inherited a collection of recordings of Mark's voice made for playing on an Edison Bell cylinder phonograph. According to Francis, Nipper would look at the phonograph with amusement and intrigue when these recordings were played, as if looking for the source of his master's voice. Nipper died in 1895 and three years later Francis decided to paint the famous picture of him looking quizzically into the horn of the phonograph. The painting was originally called 'Dog Looking at and Listening to a Phonograph', not a particularly catchy title. Francis had the idea that he would sell the painting to the company who made the phonograph as perhaps they may have a use for it. However, they were not interested and Francis was unsuccessful in finding another buyer. He changed the title to 'His Master's Voice' and in 1899 Francis finally found a buyer; the new Gramophone Company said they would take it if he changed the Edison machine to a newer model. Francis complied and received £50 for the painting and £50 for the copyright to the image.

The image of Nipper was used on products and advertising all over the world, especially in America where several companies used it. In Europe the company who acquired the Gramophone Company was EMI, whose retail arm is called HMV.

'His Master's Voice'. (Library of Congress)

Below: Nipper's plaque and street sign. (Anne Bevis)

Nipper wasn't famous during his lifetime. When he died in 1895 he was quietly laid to rest in a park on Clarence Street, Kingston-upon-Thames. A bank now occupies the site; however, a plaque resides inside the bank to commemorate the final resting place of the famous dog beneath the building. In 2010 a small street near his final resting place was named 'Nipper Alley'.

So when you next pass a HMV store and you see Nipper, think of the little white dog that started this story.

In 1899 at 126 Piccadilly
Francis Barraud
completed his famous painting
of 'Nipper' that became
known as
His Master's Voice

British Plaque Trust

Royal Kingston NIPPER ALLEY

67 | Suffragettes

The women's suffrage movement in Britain, which started in the late nineteenth century but reached its zenith in the early twentieth century, had many political and social connotations. At this time no woman had the right to vote in elections and the movement's aim was to remedy this in line with the voting rights of men, which, before the First World War, were not universal.

Those who took part in the suffrage movement did so in many different ways, both peacefully and militantly.

After the defeat of the first Women's Suffrage Bill in 1897, local groups came together to form the National Union of Women's Suffrage Societies (NUWSS). The campaigners in this organisation were known as suffragists and were non-militant, using traditional campaigning methods such as petitions and the lobbying of parliament to promote their message.

In 1903 the Women's Social and Political Union (WSPU) was formed, which was the militant section of the movement. Acting by the motto 'Deeds not words', these 'suffragettes' would disrupt meetings, chain themselves to railings and also use other violent techniques.[168] This often led to them being forcibly removed, and one suffragette, Helen Ogston, took a dogwhip hidden in her skirts to protect herself. Suffragettes were often imprisoned for their actions and started hunger strikes during their incarceration, which again prompted more publicity.

'A Worker for the Cause'. A little white terrier wears a placard urging 'Votes for Women', 1912. (Mary Evans Picture Library)

In 1911 the national census was taken and many campaigners used it as a way to voice their beliefs. Many household schedules, which was where information about the people living there were included, were spoiled or not completed. Resisters also refused to pay tax, such as Elizabeth Knight, who persistently evaded paying her dog licence, and Janet Legate Bunten, who was fined and then imprisoned for ten days for keeping a dog without a licence.

Animals were also enlisted into the cause, with many women taking their dogs with them on marches and dressing them up or using them to hold up pro-suffrage signage. Animals were often depicted on both pro- and anti-suffrage postcards and propaganda. The most popular animals were cats and dogs, with cats representing suffragettes and dogs standing for those against the vote. One example depicts a muzzled sad-looking dog with the caption 'THE VOTE. WHEN THEY GET IT.'

A suffragette dog with a pipe and spectacles. (©The March of the Women Collection/ Mary Evans Picture Library)

Who Said Votes for Women !!!

At the outbreak of the First World War, however, most put aside their differences and worked tirelessly on the home front and abroad for the war effort. The work of many of the societies was published in the local and national press. In September 1914, just weeks after the declaration of war, the *Mid-Sussex Times* reported the following:

The Haywards Heath Branch of the Central Sussex Women's Suffrage Society has decided to suspend its ordinary suffrage work for the present, in order to devote its energies to relief work at this crisis in our national affairs. The members, as an organised body of women, offered their services to the local Relief Committee by letter at its first meeting.[169]

After the war, under the terms of The Representation of the People Act 1918, all men over the age of 21 were entitled to vote, as well as women over 30 years of age, subject to some further restrictions.

68 | Swansea Jack

In the 1930s a black retriever became the saviour of those who fell in the River Tawe in Swansea. For seven years he responded to cries of help from those in the water and pulled them to safety. The dog became known as Swansea Jack and his exploits were reported in the newspapers, although his first rescue of a young boy went unreported. The number that Swansea Jack saved is not clear as reports differ from twenty-seven to twenty-nine; however, it was certainly a noteworthy number.

In 1936 Jack was awarded the 'Bravest Dog of the Year' award by the *Star* newspaper. In the *Gloucester Citizen* it was reported in July of the same year that he had made his twenty-sixth rescue from the Swansea Docks. A fisherman attempting to retrieve his line fell into the dock and, on hearing the cries of passers-by, Swansea Jack came to the dock, jumped in and brought the man to safety. Jack was awarded many medals and cups for his bravery from societies and individuals from all around the country.

Swansea Jack. (Rhodri77, CC BY-SA 3.0)

It was only just over a year later, however, that the newspapers were reporting the death of Swansea Jack, after he ate rat poison. As testament to the importance and the place Jack had in the hearts of Swansea residents, he was buried on the promenade and a memorial was paid for by public subscription. The memorial can still be seen on the promenade near the rugby ground.

69 | Lassie

Although Lassie is often viewed as an American hero dog, her inclusion here can be justified as the author of the original story, Eric Knight, was born in Yorkshire, England. The story of Lassie was originally published in the *Saturday Evening Post* in the USA in 1938 before being expanded into a successful novel, *Lassie Come Home*, in 1940. The original story was about Lassie finding her way home over a huge distance to her friend Joe, the boy of the story.

A Rough Collie like Lassie. (Nikolai Tsvetkov, Shutterstock)

The rough collie is readily described as the 'Lassie' dog and makes it an easily recognisable breed. The long coat of this breed make it a very glamorous-looking dog; however, at its heart, like all collies, it is a working dog, although its use as such is limited, as other breeds of collie are favoured. The author, Eric Knight, and his second wife reportedly bred collies on their ranch.

Eric Knight took American citizenship shortly before his death, which was in 1943 in a plane crash while serving in the US Army. The success of the novel led to a 1943 film adaptation and numerous TV series, which brought Lassie to audiences all over the world.

Every Lassie has been portrayed by a descendant of the dog in the original film, who was called Pal. Today, this line of Lassie descendants is said to be on a parallel with those of another famous dog star: Rin Tin Tin. The descendants of these two famous dogs have often met over the years and share a special spot in our childhoods and in the canine film star hall of fame.

70 | The Famous Five

In 1942 The Famous Five was born when Enid Blyton's *Five on a Treasure Island* was published. There are a total of twenty-one books in the series about the adventures of the characters Julian, Dick, Anne, George and Timmy while on their school holidays. The stories were published between 1942 and 1963; by 1953 the series had already sold over 6 million copies.

Enid Blyton was born in 1897 in East Dulwich, after which her family moved to Beckenham in Kent where her two brothers were born. She was not allowed to keep pets as a child, which she made up for when she was older. One of her most famous was Bobs, a fox terrier, and she wrote pieces about family life as seen through his eyes.

In The Famous Five books, the children's canine companion, Timmy, belongs to George (aka Georgina), the tomboy of the group. George and Anne, who is the youngest and sister of Julian and Dick, go to the same boarding school and are very lucky to go to an establishment that allows pets to accompany them to school. Their companion Timmy is faithful, clever and loyal and George is fiercely protective of him. Originally George's parents told her she couldn't keep her dog, but they changed their minds by the end of the first book.

In *Five on a Hike Together*, the girls (although George would hate to be called so) go to the school's kennels to tell Timmy about their plans for the October half term. As the girls approached the kennel:

> He heard their foot-steps at once and began to bark excitedly. He scraped at the gate of the kennel yard, wishing for the thousandth time that he could find out how to open it. He flung himself onto the two girls, licking and pawing and barking.[170]

They tell Timmy of their plans and just like many of our own canine companions, 'Timmy seemed to understand every word'.[171]

While on their hike the five travel through Coney Copse, where Timmy is surrounded by the object of his favourite pastime – rabbits. When Timmy gets stuck down a large rabbit hole after chasing them, the children pull him out by his legs.[172]

If the group is ever in trouble, Timmy is always ready to stand up for them and growl at any adults that stand in the way of their adventures or of them discovering the truth. What is endearing about The Famous Five is that Timmy actually forms an integral part of the group, and is not just a token companion. His worth is measured in his clear investment in the group's adventures and the help that he gives.

Vintage Famous Five books featuting Timmy the dog. (www.vintagecobweb.com)

71 | Dogs at Home in the Blitz

On the outbreak of war a national committee was set up to provide help and advice to the British public. The National Air Raid Precautions Animals Committee produced a pamphlet in 1939, which unfortunately caused thousands of pet owners to rush to have their pets euthanised. The advice said that pets should be found a safe place, preferably in the country in case of bombing, and if this couldn't be found, the kindest thing was to have them put to sleep. During the first year of the war Blue Cross, just one animal charity, cared for, treated, found new homes for or destroyed 152,236 animals.[173] And in 1942 a further 44,450 dogs were received, collected, treated, looked after or found new homes by Blue Cross.[174]

The Blitz was more distressing and terrifying for animals than it was for humans, as they had no understanding of the wailing of the siren, the vibrations of bombs hitting the earth or the destruction all around them. Despite the confusion that many animals felt during the Blitz, many of them worked hard and courageously during the war on the home front. Some helped to locate casualties from destroyed houses after air raids, leading rescue teams to their locations. The subject of animals on the home front is expertly covered in Claire Campbell's *Bonzo's War: Animals Under Fire 1939–1945*.

In light of the work that dogs performed, it is necessary to mention some of those who were awarded the Dickin Medal for bravery (the medal itself will be discussed further in its own chapter). A quick count on the PDSA website makes a total of nineteen dogs who were awarded the Dickin Medal for their activities during the Second World War, and seven of those were dogs who aided the location and rescue of people at home.[175]

One example of the many that could be recounted here is of Rex, a German shepherd. Rex was in training as a search dog to locate trapped people under debris when in January 1945 he was called upon, despite the fact he hadn't finished his training, to work at a bombsite in Lambeth. When he arrived he began digging at an area where a path had been cleared and since been well trodden. Putting this down to his lack of experience, he was moved away. However, they had underestimated Rex, and when he continued to try and return to the area the men began digging and eventually found two bodies.[176]

On another occasion, Rex was taken to a factory that was on fire. He searched the area until he had to be taken away due to the risk of the building collapsing, and had to be pulled off the site as he refused to leave his work willingly. On returning later he found five casualties within four minutes.[177] Rex's citation reads:

For outstanding good work in the location of casualties in burning buildings. Undaunted by smouldering debris, thick smoke, intense heat and jets of water from fire hoses, this dog displayed uncanny intelligence and outstanding determination in his efforts to follow up any scent which led him to a trapped casualty.[178]

The willingness of these dogs and others to risk their own safety in order to carry out their job is astounding and the Dicken Medal citations provide many amazing stories of their courage and bravery. It can only be hoped that the love and care that we humans give our dogs is in some way deserving of their unquestioning loyalty.

'Rip' the dog helps this air raid precautions warden to search amongst rubble and debris following an air raid in Poplar. (Imperial War Museum)

Emile Corteil and Glen

In preparation for D-Day on 6 June 1944, during the hours before the assault on the beaches, many paratroops were transported into Normandy via glider aeroplane and by parachuting from planes high over the sleepy villages of France. The men of the Parachute Regiment helped clear the way for those who would storm the beaches later that morning.

Among those who jumped from planes and silently glided to earth by parachute was Emile Corteil from Watford, Hertfordshire, of A Company, 9th (Essex) Parachute Battalion. What made his role more unusual was that he was the company dog handler. Dogs accompanied many of the airborne troops as rescue dogs to search out the wounded, act as sentries and as guards. Glen, the company's dog, parachuted down on his own and would have been released by Emile as soon as he touched the ground. Then his harness would have been adjusted to the working position and they would have begun their work.

It is not known exactly what happened to Emile and Glen, but the two were found lying dead together. They are buried with many other men of the Parachute Regiment who were killed in the hours before and after the D-Day assault in Ranville Cemetery, Normandy, France. The inscription on the tomb reads:

Had you known our boy you would have loved him too. Glen his parachute dog was killed with him.

Omaha Beach on D-Day. (Everett Historical, Shutterstock)

At Saint Catherine, Canada, a police dog parachutes with his owner. (Mary Evans Picture Library)

73 | Just Nuisance

Many of the stories of mascots are those from army units; however, there is certainly one dog who is well known to those of the Royal Navy past and present: Just Nuisance.

A Great Dane, likely to be Just Nuisance, with sailors in Cape Town. (Australian War Memorial Collection)

As his name suggests, he was a nuisance, not only because of his size but also because of his habit for resting fully out on the gangplank. Nuisance was a Great Dane, which is a large breed in itself, but he was extremely large at nearly 2m tall when standing upright on his hind legs. Details of Nuisance's early life are patchy, but it is believed he was born in Rodenbosch, near Cape Town, South Africa in April 1937. His owner moved to Simon's Town to run the United Service Institute there, where Nuisance became a favourite with the men, who would feed him and then be followed back to the dockyard by him, where he would sit on the decks of any ships moored there.

Problems began to hinder Nuisance when his travels further and further afield with the sailors eventually took him on to other modes of transport, especially trains, where he would be discovered and ejected by the conductors. Nuisance's owner, Benjamin Chaney, was warned by the railway company that if Nuisance didn't stop taking train rides or start paying his fares, they would have him destroyed. Many of the servicemen who knew Nuisance offered to pay his fares or provide him with a season ticket, but someone came up with an even better idea – to enlist him in the Royal Navy, therefore entitling him to free travel. Nuisance became the only dog ever enlisted into the Royal Navy. His official date of entry was 25 August 1939 and he did a lot of work for the morale of servicemen during the Second World War. Postcards of him were also sold to raise money for the war effort.

These are the details from Just Nuisance's enlistment form:

Christian Name: Just

Surname: Nuisance

Trade: Bone Crusher

Religious Denomination: Scrounger (later updated to Canine Divinity League)[179]

Nuisance was even promoted from ordinary seaman to able seaman. He was not a perfect sailor, however, and his conduct sheet shows that he had gone Absent Without Leave (AWOL), refused to leave the pub at closing time and also fought with the mascots of other ships that visited. He often attended official functions as he became a celebrity and even had a wedding to a female Great Dane, Adinda, from which union five puppies were born.

He was discharged from the Royal Navy on 1 January 1944 after a motor accident had injured him, causing him to be slowly paralysed. He was put to sleep on 1 April 1944, thought to have been his 7th birthday. The following day he was buried with full naval honours, wrapped in a naval ensign with a gun salute and a bugler sounding the Last Post. A headstone marks his resting place on Red Hill at Klaver Camp.[180]

News of his death spread far and wide; the *Hastings and St Leonards Observer* marked his passing on 8 April with a photograph of Nuisance with a local man who was at a convalescent camp in Simon's Town. All of Just Nuisance's records are now at the Simon's Town Museum, along with his collar and photographs. A statue on Jubilee Square was erected to his memory.

A Great Dane like Just Nuisance. (Vivienstock, Shutterstock)

74 | The Dickin Medal

This award is given to animals who have shown great bravery or devotion to duty during conflict and is more often known as the Animals' Victoria Cross. The medal was instituted in 1943 by Maria Dickin CBE, the founder of the Peoples Dispensary for Sick Animals (PDSA).

The Dickin Medal has been awarded sixty-seven times since 1943: the recipients include thirty-two pigeons, thirty-one dogs, three horses and one cat.[181] While all of their stories are well worth reading – they can be found on the PDSA website – the boundaries of this book focus our attention on the dogs to whom this award has been bestowed. Nine awards have been made to dogs for their work and bravery in conflicts since the Second World War and some of the more recent recipients are well known due to media coverage of the award.

Rip was awarded the Dickin Medal for bravery in 1945. (Imperial War Museum)

One of the most recent recipients was Sasha, a Labrador who searched for arms and explosives in Afghanistan. She was with her handler Lance Corporal Ken Rowe with the 2nd Battalion, the Parachute Regiment, when they were killed in a Taliban ambush.[182] Sasha's citation reads, 'For outstanding gallantry and devotion to duty while assigned to 2nd Battalion, The Parachute Regiment, in Afghanistan 2008.'[183] She was posthumously awarded the medal on 21 May 2014.

Dogs involved in other, less well-known conflicts include a group of dogs from the RAF anti-terrorist tracker dogs who took part in the jungle conflict in Malaysia. The nature of the conflict necessitated patrols of the jungle, and four dogs were taken by the troops: Bobbie, Jasper, Lassie and Lucky.[184] The thick

The Dickin Medal. (Sergeant Adrian Harlen, Defence Imagery, Open Government Licence)

jungle and immense heat made it a difficult place for both men and dogs to operate, but all the dogs were helpful in identifying any enemy soldiers near them while on patrol, as well as tracking any who ran off. The Dickin Medal was only awarded in 2007 and the dog to whom it was given for service in the Malayan Emergency was decided by ballot. Lucky, a German shepherd and the only one of the four to survive the conflict, was picked.[185] Lucky's citation reads:

For the outstanding gallantry and devotion to duty of the RAF Police anti-terrorist tracker dog team, comprising Bobbie, Jasper, Lassie and Lucky, while attached to the Civil Police and several British Army regiments including the Coldstream Guards, 2nd Battalion Royal Scots Guards and the Ghurkhas during the Malaya Campaign. Bobbie, Jasper, Lassie and Lucky displayed exceptional determination and life-saving skills during the Malaya Campaign. The dogs and their handlers were an exceptional team, capable of tracking and locating the enemy by scent despite unrelenting heat and an almost impregnable jungle. Sadly, three of the dogs lost their lives in the line of duty: only Lucky survived to the end of the conflict.[186]

In September 2014 the first PDSA Honorary Dickin Medal was given to Warrior, a cavalry horse who served during the First World War. No such award existed during Warrior's time and many deeds of bravery by all animals such as horses, mules, pigeons, donkeys and dogs have gone unrecognised. The award made to Warrior was intended to honour all the animals that served during war.[187]

75 | The Second World War

At the end of the First World War, the War Dog School was liquidated as it was not thought necessary to keep a peacetime training centre in operation. However, in 1939, on the eve of the outbreak of war, Colonel Richardson could again foresee the need for trained dogs to aid the armed forces.

Although Colonel Richardson provided a great deal of assistance in the training and information about war dogs, he didn't take the lead as he had done previously, due to his age (by the outbreak of the Second World War he was in his mid-70s). Instead Richardson suggested a friend of his who had worked under him at the War Dog School – another military man, named Major James Baldwin. Baldwin was one of the first to import the German shepherd (or the Alsatian, as the British have persisted in naming the breed, despite being the only ones in the world to do so). Baldwin, like Richardson, could see how important dogs could be in the conflict and duly starting training them even without the authority from his commanders.

Those who could see the potential in dogs began to set up a Volunteer Dog Trained Reserve in collaboration with The Kennel Club, RAF, navy and army, as well as chiefs of police from England and Wales. Its aim was to create a register of owners and trained dogs who could offer their dogs for immediate use by the War Office on short notice should they call on them or if there was a national emergency.

In 1940 it was finally decided to start a small operation that would provide dogs for patrol and messenger purposes. Just the same as in the First World War, a public appeal was made to ask for dogs to be donated to the school. Only a small number were expected; however, 7,000 dogs were offered within the first two weeks. The RSPCA helped to recruit dogs but received backlash for role in helping to send dogs overseas where they could be harmed or killed. However, the alternative was just as threatening, as many pets, including thousands of dogs, had been put down due to fear of bombing. Therefore suitable dogs were in short supply and other charities began to help by identifying owners who wished to donate animals they

could not otherwise keep and by examining these dogs.

After the patrol and messenger dog training had proven effective, dogs began to be trained in other tasks, including replacing men at depots and ammunition stores. These dogs were often deployed with servicemen in the Corps of Military Police for guarding strategically important places, where they could be used to detect the scent of an unauthorised human and track them down. Many humorous tales can be found regarding

Major Richardson, the man behind British dog teams, with some of his British Red Cross dogs. (Library of Congress, LC-DIG-ggbain-19164)

the use of these dogs who undoubtedly did a fantastic job of keeping these vulnerable places safe – perhaps sometimes too safe, as the following story relates:

A V.P. [Vulnerable Point Section] dog was with his handler, patrolling the perimeter of a Broadcasting Station. It was a very sultry evening and an announcer who had a break in the programme of a few minutes came out into the night air for relaxation. The dog, however, caught his scent and the handler, releasing the dog who was persisting that there was some unauthorised person about, suddenly heard a scream. On going forward to discover what had happened he found the announcer half-way up a pylon with the dog sitting threateningly below. The B.B.C. apologised later for a 'technical hitch'. The true reason however was exposed in the next morning's Press.[188]

Later, dogs were trained to detect non-metallic landmines and anti-personnel mines. Their descendants today work along with their handlers in extremely dangerous situations all over the globe. Only twenty to thirty minutes of this job could be carried out at one time due to the intense concentration needed by both dog and handler. It was also found that a fresh minefield needed to be used every day in training as the dogs would use their memory instead of their noses. The dogs worked in platoons, with three sections of four dogs and their handlers in use, and a fourth kept in reserve.

Dogs were also trained as first-aid or rescue dogs, in a similar way as they were before and during the Great War, to locate the wounded on what could be an enormous battlefield. These dogs were trained with the Airborne Divisions to accompany stretcher-bearers and had their own parachutes. On landing they would have their harness adjusted, which gave them the 'on duty' command, and would then work in a given area searching for men in the prone position, having been trained to ignore all others. On finding a wounded man the dog would return to its handler and sit, waiting for its lead to be attached so it could take the handler to the wounded man. This undoubtedly helped morale within the troops, knowing that there was a friend in the darkness with an excellent nose, whose specific job was to find them if they were wounded.

In 1948 85-year-old Lieutenant-Colonel Richardson passed away. He had lived through both the First and Second World Wars and trained dogs for each. The life that he devoted to this work and his country was rewarded with an OBE. In *Fifty Years with Dogs*, published posthumously, Richardson ends with a tribute to the dog, which fittingly serves as the conclusion at the end of this book.

76 | Judy

The story of Judy, a brave and courageous dog during the Second World War, is both sad and happy. She experienced one of the worst hardships any human could have endured in a Japanese internment camp, and amazingly survived and continued to live with her beloved owner.

Judy was a liver-and-white English Pointer who was bred in the Shanghai Kennels in 1936. Pointers are a traditional gundog breed used in Britain for indicating the presence of game. It is now considered a British breed; however, its origins are thought to be in Spain.

Judy first served as the mascot of a Royal Navy ship, HMS *Gnat*, and later HMS *Grasshopper*. During the Malay–Singapore campaign, *Grasshopper* was forced to beach, marooning its company.[189] Eventually the sailors were captured by the Japanese and taken to the Gloergoer prisoner-of-war camp at Medan, with Judy hidden in a sack. There Judy met a fellow prisoner, Frank Williams, and the two became inseparable, sharing Williams' maggoty rations. Unfortunately Judy had no protection under law, but Williams managed to convince the camp commander to register Judy as an official prisoner of war, which would give her a measure of protection. So she became Prisoner81A, the only dog to be enrolled as a POW. Judy's role as a companion helped to boost the morale of many men, and gave her owner a reason to live through horrendous experiences. Judy did excellent work alerting the prisoners to dangerous insects and reptiles that found their way into the camp, as well as attempting to distract the guards while they were punishing prisoners.[190]

After her release, she was smuggled on to a ship to England where on arrival she had to endure six months' quarantine at the RSPCA Kennels at Hackbridge in Surrey. The two became celebrities and Williams was awarded the PDSA White Cross of St Giles for his care of Judy through such trying times.[191] Judy was awarded the Dickin Medal on 2 May 1946 and the citation reads:

For magnificent courage and endurance in Japanese prison camps which helped to maintain morale among her fellow prisoners, and also for saving many lives through her intelligence and watchfulness.[192]

Frank Williams took Judy home with him to Portsmouth where he lived before moving to Tanzania for a job and, of course, Judy went with him. Two years later it was found she had a tumour and at the age of 13 she was put to sleep.[193] An elaborate memorial was put on her grave by Frank with the following epitaph:

Judy sits up and listens to a sailor's commands on the deck of HMS *Grasshopper*. (Imperial War Museum)

In memory of
Jude DM Canine VC
Breed English Pointer
Born Shanghai February 1936, Died February 1950
Wounded 14 February 1942
Bombed and sunk HMS *Grasshopper*
Lingga Archipelago 14 Februar 1942.
Torpedoed SS *Van Waerwijk*
Malacca Strait 26 June 1943
Japanese prisoner of war March 1942-August 1945
Chine Ceylon Java England Egypt Burma
Singapore Malaya Sumatra E Africa
They Also Served[194]

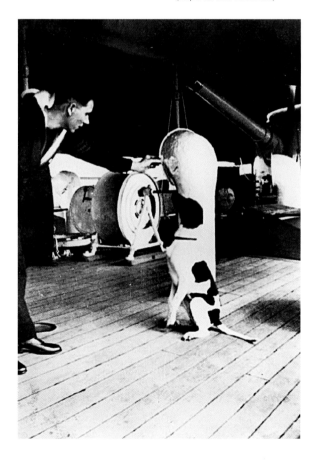

77 | Blue Peter

For millions of children and adults who have grown up watching Blue Peter, one of the outstanding memories of whichever era of the show you watched will be the pets. From cats and dogs to tortoises and parrots, many of us can remember their names and their often hilarious antics. The idea behind having pets on the show was to be able to share the experience of seeing a pet grow up, and for children who were unable to have pets of their own to learn about caring for them.

For most of use, the fondest memories will be of the dogs who accompanied the presenters in the studio as well as out and about. You can even distinguish the era of Blue Peter you watched by the pets' names that you remember. There were also many guide dog puppies in training who popped in and out over the years.

Here are the names of the Blue Peter dogs and the years they were on the show:
Petra: 1962–1977
Patch: 1965–1971
Shep: 1971–1978
Goldie: 1978–1986
Bonnie: 1986–1999
Mabel: 1996–2010
Lucy: 1998–2010
Meg: 1999–2006
Barney: 2009–2013

The mongrel Petra, since her death, has been a controversial member of the cast. It was recently uncovered that the original puppy died shortly after its first appearance and was replaced to prevent upsetting the show's young audience. The replacement, which was named Petra by viewers, went on to be the longest-serving Blue Peter dog, spending fourteen years in front on the camera. (The overall longest-serving Blue Peter pet was George the tortoise, with twenty-two years on the show.) When Peter Purves joined the show he became Petra's handler both on and off screen. There is even a statue of Petra in the Blue Peter garden in Salford commemorating her.

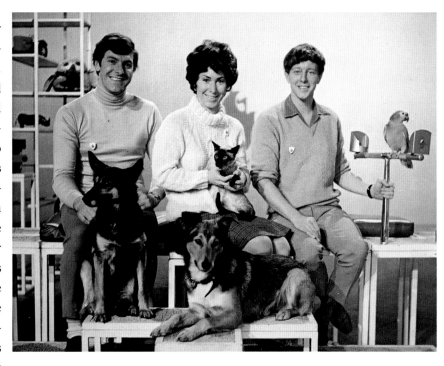

Peter Purves, Valerie Singleton, John Noakes, Jason the cat, Petra and Patch the dogs and Barney the parrot. Blue Peter 1969. (BBC)

Shep, who joined the show in 1971, was brought in to replace Patch, Petra's son who predeceased her. He was looked after by John Noakes who had also been Patch's handler. For a whole generation of viewers, Shep became famous for his excited outbursts in and outside of the studio and Noakes' catchphrase 'Get down Shep' was just as famous; The Barron Knights even penned a song with the catchphrase as its title in 1978.

It became tradition for exiting presenters to take home the dogs whom they had cared for during their time on the show. Many Blue Peter dogs have had long and happy retirements with their former colleagues or, in Shep's case, continued to share the limelight with John in 'Go with Noakes'.

78 | Sooty and Sweep

Sooty was created in 1948 by Harry Corbett when he bought the puppet from a stall in Blackpool for his son Matthew. Originally the puppet was all yellow but was given black ears to make him stand out on TV, hence his name.

A vintage Sweep puppet. (Sarah Rider)

Corbett and Sooty won the *Britain's Got Talent* of their day in BBC's *Talent Night*, competing in heats and then a final with the winner decided by public vote. The pair then became regulars on the Saturday Special until 1955 when *The Sooty Show* began airing. Various reworkings of the series saw the puppets working in a shop, hotel and a holiday camp.

Sweep is a long-eared grey dog who joined Sooty as a companion on the show in 1957 and is most memorable for his high-pitched squeak. Other members of the cast, mainly Soo the panda, translate what Sweep says for the audience. Sweep's antics, and those of his large family who have appeared over the years, provide a comical addition to the show. In October 1989 'Sweep's Family' aired and introduced us to Sweep's brothers: Swoop, Swipe and Swap are all identical and the only way of telling them apart is by their different coloured collars. The show is the longest-running children's TV series.

Housed at Leeds Castle in the dog collar collection is one of Sweep's own collars placed amongst those of other dogs. Sweep's collar is made of tartan ribbon and was worn by him from the 1980s onwards until it was donated to the collection at Sooty's 50th birthday party.

79 | Queen Elizabeth II

It is well known that Queen Elizabeth II has a love of animals, but especially dogs; her preferred breed is the Welsh corgi, of which there are two types, the Cardigan and the Pembroke. It would seem that all of the reigning monarchs and their families have had a love of dogs of varying breeds: the spaniels of the Stuarts, the pugs of William and Mary, and the corgis of the Windsors.

As a young princess, Elizabeth's family owned many dogs and it was during her childhood that the first corgi, a Pembroke called Dookie, was introduced to the mix.[195] Dookie was bad tempered and often bit visitors who got too close. A book was published in 1936 called *The Princesses and Their Dogs* by Michael Chance, which contained many photographs of the royal family and their dogs.

The Cardigan Corgi.
(Vivienstock, Shutterstock)

When at home, the queen is usually followed by a number of corgis that are often the only accompaniment on walks in the grounds. One biographer of the queen has written that 'wherever The Queen goes in the Palace, her corgis go with her. They are inseparable and are rarely out of her sight unless she has a formal duty.'[196]

It is said that during dress fittings, where her beloved dogs are also in attendance, the assistants have to be careful to pick up any small pins that could injure one of the dogs and also work around them as they lay on the floor. It is rumoured that the queen carries a small magnet to run over the floor to pick up any small bits of metal that could hurt a paw.[197]

Opposite: A Welsh Corgi. (Degtyaryov Andrew, Shutterstock)

Right: Vintage postcard showing Princess Margaret and Princess Elizabeth with Queen Elizabeth the Queen Mother and a pet corgi. (The History Press)

Below: Queen Elizabeth's father, George VI, with his corgi. (Mary Evans Picture Library)

The Cardigan breed of corgi is thought to be the elder of the two with a history going back to 1200.[198] Although the two closely resemble each other, there are some differences that have become more prominent in recent years, and the two were split officially in the 1930s. The Cardigan variety has slightly larger ears, with any colour being acceptable as long as white doesn't predominate, and also has a long tail, which is unusual for a low-set dog. The dog has been known as the yard dog because the length from its nose to end of tail is a Welsh yard.

As with the dogs of previous members of the royal family, many of Queen Elizabeth II's dogs are commemorated at Sandringham Palace.

80 | Cartoon Dogs

Most of us will have a favourite cartoon character and many of them will be dogs. There are far too many beloved animated dogs to mention them all here. Some of these characters span certain decades of children's television and so are only iconic depending on the generation; however, many of them have been classics for their unmistakable characteristics, whether it be their laugh, crazy shenanigans or helping us to read. Although, not always created in Britain, they were keenly watched and emulated here and therefore worthy of inclusion. Here are just a few to stir some memories:

Spotty Dog: The Woodentops

The Woodentops was part of the Watch with Mother group of shows and was a black-and-white string puppet creation portraying family life in the country. The main characters were a family living on a farm and included Spotty Dog, 'The very biggest spotty dog you ever did see'. The series ran for a relatively short time from 1955–57.

Dougal: The Magic Roundabout

Created in France in the early 1960s and first broadcast in the UK in October 1965,[199] *The Magic Roundabout* continued to be a favourite for generations of children thanks to reruns into the 1990s. Dougal wasn't in the original show's line-up but appeared after the first few years and the cast continued to grow with Ermintrude the cow and Dylan the rabbit. In the show, Dougal was a character that seemed to slide smoothly rather than walk anywhere, with a love of sugar lumps and a mass of straight hair that gave him the appearance of a Skye terrier. Originally the series aired just before the evening news; however, it was later moved to a more child-friendly time – for which the BBC received numerous complaints from adult viewers.[200] More recently, a fully animated film was shown in cinemas in 2005, bringing Zebedee's weird and wonderful world back to life.

Dill the Dog: The Herbs

Herbidacious! *The Herbs* was the creation of Michael Bond, author of the Paddington Bear stories loved all over the world. Two series of the show were made; in the first the animal characters had no voices and Dill communicated via barking; however, by the second series the characters were given voices of their own. Dill was a lively character, which I'm sure many dog owners could relate to! He was the opposite of Parsley the lion's slow and more considered temperament.

Muttley: The Wacky Races

An American import from the Hanna-Barbera studio, *The Wacky Races* featured a large number of cartoon characters, all with their own stories and personalities. The sniggering Muttley accompanied Dick Dastardly in his often ridiculous and fiendish attempts to win the race. The pair also appeared in their own show, *Dastardly and Muttley in Their Flying Machines*, which is better known as Stop the Pigeon thanks to the theme music. Here Muttley donned an aviator's scarf and goggles. Muttley even got his own segments in the series *The Magnificent Muttley*, where he would daydream about finding himself in different and often historical situations.

Spot: Spot the Dog

Spot was a dog who helped children to explore the world and learn to read. Based on the original books by Eric Hill and then adapted into a TV series, multiple video releases were made and loved by young children. Learning and exploring with Spot and his family and friends is fondly remembered by children of the 1980s.

Other famous cartoon dogs include Scooby Doo, Pluto and Goofy, Astro Jetson, Mr Peabody, Odie from *Garfield*, Santa's Little Helper and, of course, Clifford the Big Red Dog. Many of these characters' cartoons have made comebacks in recent years such as *The Magic Roundabout*, *Mr Peabody & Sherman*, *Garfield* and, most recently, *Peanuts*. Therefore for those of us who have now grown into adults, there is another excuse to return to our childhoods and revisit some of our most favourite cartoon dogs once again.

Spot the Dog puppet.
(Chris West)

81 | Collies

The full complement of collie breeds rival the spaniels in numbers and also in the public's devotion to them. Collies have not only been used for centuries by shepherds and farmers to tend to their flocks but are now also family pets, with boundless energy and cleverness to match.

Bearded Collie. (Kazlouski Siarhei)

The Border collie is probably the best-known breed of this group and possibly the most popular. The name derives from the dogs' original role in the hills around the border areas of Scotland, England and Wales, where they worked with sheep. Border collies are now used throughout the country and are highly appreciated in professional circles, as they are extremely clever, quick to learn and enjoy challenges in a work environment. For this reason they are a clear choice for police and rescue services. Traditionally working dogs, it is only more recently that Border collies have become a feature of show ring competitions.[201]

Rough collies are discussed in the chapter that tells of their most famous ancestor, Lassie.

Bearded collies have only recently become more common, with their current characteristics created by a pairing in the 1940s. Before this as a breed it seems to have seen very little popularity outside of Scotland and in Hugh Dalziel's book he only devotes a quarter of a page to bearded collies.

The one variation of the collie that seems at odds with the others is the smooth collie; its coat is short and flat but its characteristics mirror the rough collie.

Collies are a breed valued for friendship and loyalty, their readiness and eagerness to work hard, and their capacity to learn. They have made the transition from working dog to pet, while still being highly regarded in both spheres.

Opposite: A group of collies, showing some of the different colours available. (Ksenia Raykova)

Left: 1876 sheepdog trials at Alexandra Palace. (©Illustrated London News Ltd/Mary Evans Picture Library)

Below, left: Collie herding sheep. (Mikkel Bigandt, Shutterstock)

Below, right: Watercolour portrait of a rough collie. (Malcolm Greensmith ©Adrian Bradbury/Mary Evans)

82 | The Dog Licence

In the UK, dog owners were required by law to purchase a dog licence for their pets. This law was repealed in 1987 – it was thought that only half of dog owners purchased a licence in the final years of the law. Previously, the threat of losing a pet if they were caught by the police or a dog catcher – who would have the animal destroyed if they were not claimed and the licence paid – obliged owners to pay what was for many a hefty sum. In its last year the licence was 37.5p, which was the equivalent of *7s 6d* in predecimal money. It was always due on 1 January. Not all dogs needed to have a licence and those who used their dog for work purposes could apply for exemption.

One charity, Our Dumb Friends' League' (now Blue Cross) established in 1897, turned its attention from caring for the horses who provided the main forms of transport in London to the plight of dogs too. While Blue Cross had many 'funds' that helped to fundraise and then pay for different aspects of their work, one was specifically aimed at helping those who found it difficult to pay their dog's licence. Originally this fund was set up to pay for the licences of dogs belonging to men fighting with the army reservists in the Boer War (1900–03), and whose families found it difficult to afford without their main breadwinner. In the First World War this problem became more commonplace and the families of those who had gone to war often appealed to the charity for help. The shelters and hospitals of Blue Cross cared for many of these dogs themselves while their owners were away and, in 1918, 1,771 licences were paid for by its Dog Licence Fund. In 1919 the fund paid for 1,032 licences.[202]

At the end of the war, when many servicemen had found comfort and solace in pets found abroad to whom they had formed a strong bond, the thought of having to leave them behind was too much and many attempted to conceal their animals on the journey home. The work of the charity in this respect is covered in the chapter 'Blue Cross in the First World War'.

Dog licensing had more repercussions than perhaps some families not having pets or forcing them to apply to Blue Cross if they couldn't afford it. When the licence was enforced many dogs were handed into animal shelters or simply let loose to fend for themselves. In 1938 the Blue Cross annual report stated that 50 per cent more dogs were received at the time when the licence payment was due.[203]

One particular example from the Blue Cross records is the issue the charity had over a situation in Ramsgate, Kent. The mayor of that town fined a man for not having a licence and went on to say that because the man was unemployed, he should not have a dog. The charity responded that in its opinion the dogs of the poor were sometimes better cared for than 'many a pampered pet of the rich'. A quote from the information provided by Blue Cross on the work of its Dog Licence Fund is very relevant here:

Vintage licence from the 1920s, when a licence for one dog cost 7s 6d. (The History Press)

> To build up a nation of persons who did not know the love and affection an animal can give was detrimental to animals as a whole, as well as being detrimental to the nation.

It also stated that the league failed to see why a poor person should be deprived of his friend.[204]

Charities such as the RSPCA, PDSA, Battersea and many other local organisations have been there for our pets for over 100 years. The work they do in caring for, but also on behalf of, our pets is very important and long may it continue.

83 | Dog Memorials

The animal cemeteries at Hyde Park, Preston Manor near Brighton and, of course, the memorial stone at Sandringham are covered in various chapters within this book. However, there are other memorials around Britain which mark the part that dogs have played in human lives.

In the grand Chichester Cathedral in West Sussex, many beautiful and ornate memorials, stones, effigies and windows can be marvelled at and enjoyed. One installation stands out not only for its beautiful depiction of love between husband and wife even in death, but also for its appreciation of a dog. Between the north aisle and the nave sits a fourteenth-century stone effigy of the Earl of Arundel, Richard Fitzalan and his wife the Countess of Arundel, Lady Eleanor Plantagenet.[205] The couple died in 1376 and 1372 respectively and are portrayed holding hands. The effigies were brought to national attention by the poet Philip Larkin (1922–85) when he wrote a poem called *The Arundel Tomb* describing it.

The Animals in War Memorial. (Iridescenti/ Creative Commons)

While the earl's feet rest on top of a lion, at the bottom of the countess' dress lies a dog as if it was sleeping at her feet.

A momument much more in the public consciousness is the Animals in War Memorial located at Brook Gate, Park Lane, London. It was unveiled by HRH the Princess Royal in November 2004[206] and is dedicated to all the animals that not only served in the armed forces on the home front but also to those who died through the actions of war in conflicts of the twentieth century. The monument not only has a wall made out of Portland stone, the same material used for headstones in Commonwealth Grave Commission cemeteries around the world, but also has touching sculptures of two mules, a horse and a dog. On the wall, images of the animals commemorated are carved along with the name of the memorial and a list of major donors.[207] The Animals in War Memorial is a reminder of all the animals who have been affected by warfare in the last 100 years, without whom many more humans would have died because of lack of supplies, loss of communications or being hidden under rubble.

A much older memorial, this time to a human, portrays the trade of a man and his importance to his employer even in death. In 1777 the Honourable John Gordon of Kenmore erected a tombstone in the churchyard at Kells, Galloway in Scotland to his gamekeeper John Murray. The stone is unusual for the items depicted on it, such as a powder flask, partridge, gun and dog.[208] The following epitaph is also inscribed on the stone:

Ah! John, what changes since I saw thee last –
Thy fishing and thy shooting days are past;
Bag-pipes and haut-boys thou canst sound no more,
Thy nods, grimaces, winks and pranks are o'er;
Thy harmless, queerish, incoherent talk,
Thy wild vivacity and trudging walk,
Will soon be quite forgot; thy joys on earth,
Thy snuff and glass, riddles and noisy mirth
Are vanished all; yet blessed I hope thou art,
For in thy station thou hast played thy part.

84 | Dogs in the Census

In 2011 the nation filled out its decennial census, a custom nationally undertaken (except in wartime) since 1841. This collects information relating to the population and now provides an army of family and local history researchers with one of their most important resources. A recent pet census undertaken by Petplan estimated that there are 24 million pets in the United Kingdom, 8 million of them dogs.[209] In the 2011 'human' census, 16 per cent of the population included their pets on the form; however, this is not a new phenomenon among the pet-loving British public, as records show pet owners entering their dogs on census forms over 100 years ago on the 1911 census:[210]

CASE OF CENSUS-CONSCIENCE.

Conscientious Head of Family (an old Lady, giving the paper, on Monday, to the Enumerator). "HERE IS THE PAPER, MR. ACCUMULATOR, BUT I WANT PARTICULAR TO SAY SOMETHING FOR THE INFORMATION OF HER MAJESTY, BLESS HER HEART, LIKEWISE HER FAMILY! WHICH YOU SEE IT SAYS 'SLEPT OR ABODE'—AND I WOULDN'T DECEIVE HER MAJESTY AND HER GOVERNMENT ON NO ACCOUNT, AND THE FACT IS, THAT I DIDN'T SLEEP A WINK ALL THE BLESSED NIGHT BY REASON OF A TOOTH, WHICH I HOPE YOU'LL EXPLAIN TO THE QUEEN, AND SAY I COULDN'T HAVE IT TOOK OUT ON SATURDAY, AS MY DENTIST IS OF THE JEWISH PERSUASION, WHICH I DON'T BLAME HIM FOR, QUITE THE REVERSE, BUT I AM GOING TO HIM TO-DAY TO HAVE IT EXTRICATED, AND SO PLEASE TO SAY THAT I ONLY 'ABIDED,'" &c., &c., &c., &c.

Arthur Delve from Smethwick entered his pet dog Biddy at the bottom of his form, stating that she was 'a faithfull [sic] Irish Terrier ... Magnificent Watch, a demon on Cats and Vermin' and that she was 11 years old.[211] A journalist living in Herne Hill also offered information regarding his dog, this time filling out the census form fully as per each member of his household. The forward to the entry reads:

Incidentally, we have an Airedale Terrier. I do not know whether particulars are required, but in case you want them they are:

Name: Roger; Age: 5; Marital status: unknown; years married: unknown; Children born alive: unknown but something over 100; Personal occupation: Watchdog; Industry or service with which work is connected: Looking after house; Whether employer, worker or working on own account: own account; Whether working at home: At home and outside; Birthplace: Keighley, Yorkshire.[212]

Undoubtedly, these two owners were not alone in their perception of their dogs as part of the family, and 100 years later pet owners still feel and act the same way.

Right: An Irish terrier appeared on the 1911 census, where he was listed as 'a demon on Cats and Vermin'. (Lipowski Milan, Shutterstock)

Opposite: Punch cartoon lampooning the British tendency to overshare on the census. (Wellcome Library, London)

85 | Extinct Dogs

Many breeds over the centuries have come into use or popularity for their effectiveness at carrying out certain jobs. When these are no longer fashionable many breeds have fallen into extinction, with very little documentation to describe their features or uses to a modern audience. It is not possible to cover every extinct breed, many of which we may never even know about, but it is possible to find out about those which have vanished more recently. Some of these are variations of breeds in existence today, whereas others are completely individual.

English water spaniel

When describing spaniels in his 1570 work, John Caius split the breed into two varieties; those that hunted on land and those that hunted in water. In 1800 Thomas Bewick noted three distinct varieties; the large rough water dog, the large water spaniel and the small water spaniel. All three breeds enjoyed the water and retrieving wounded game that inhabited rivers and waterways. The first type 'the large rough water dog' had webbed feet and is therefore likely to be a relative of the Newfoundland. The two water spaniels had curly coats and were excellent at swimming and retrieving waterfowl.

A Georgian illustration of a 'rough water dog', probably like a water spaniel. (Wellcome Library, London)

ROUGH WATER DOG

Hugh Dalziel, in his work on dogs in the late nineteenth century, discusses the English water spaniel as a breed still included in The Kennel Club Stud Book, although today it is no longer recognised. He suggested that the English water spaniel was much older than its Irish counterpart and commented that although the breed was not lost, it was spread thinly throughout the country. He goes on to describe its general appearance: 'strong, compact, of medium size, leggy by comparison with the Clumber, Sussex or black field spaniel, and showing much greater activity.'[213]

Although spaniels still encompass the same skills and work in the same role, the English water spaniel is no longer recognised as a distinct breed and the Irish water spaniel is the one acknowledged as a 'water spaniel'.

Tweed water spaniel

A relation of the Irish water spaniel, its native home was around the River Tweed in the Scottish Borders.

Norfolk spaniel

Dash II, a Norfolk spaniel from the late nineteenth century. (*The Dog Book*, James Watson)

There were attempts to identify the Norfolk spaniel as a distinct breed from both the Clumber and Sussex varieties, but even in the mid-nineteenth century this caused problems for commentators. It was difficult to describe the Norfolk spaniel's features in detail, as they were so close to other breeds, and being so few in number and bred widely with other spaniels made it difficult to find a breed standard.

English white terrier

The terrier breeds are well known for their varieties and also their use as vermin destroyers. The English white terrier was described as a mix of fox terrier, bull terrier and whippet.[214]

Blue Paul

Blue Paul was a type of terrier that existed mainly in Scotland. Legend says that the dog was brought to Britain by the infamous pirate Paul Jones and used for dogfighting in pits. The dog had a blue coat, which is today found in other terrier breeds, and they were judged in shows as a white version of the black-and-tan terrier.

Old English bulldog

This breed of bulldog is thought to be one of the oldest in Britain, and would have been found in ancient times fighting as war dogs. The advent of bull-baiting and dogfighting gave rise to specialised breeding to accentuate fighting capabilities in the dog pits around the country. The reason for breeding this dog is the same for its decline: the Cruelty to Animals Act in 1835 meant a decline of dogfighting so the breed was no longer in demand.

Paisley terrier

This terrier was often referred to as the Paisley Skye terrier as it was a smaller or 'toy' version of the traditional Skye terrier, being shorter in length and often half the weight.

Southern hound

When *Dogs of the British Islands* by J.H. Walsh (who wrote under the name Stonehenge) was published in 1882, this breed was already no longer in existence; the author notes that the Southern hound would not be discussed as, even though it had been previously common, it was now extinct.[215] This dog was most often described as the predecessor of the Otter hound, as well as other breeds such as harriers and bloodhounds.

These dogs, though they are no longer recognised individually and have largely been forgotten over the centuries, still have characteristics present in our breeds today.

86 | Pub Names

Dogs not only form part of our history and lives by being our companions, but they have also become integral to our art, memorials and signs; it is the latter of these that we are concerned with here. Pubs have a long tradition of being named after dogs or the sports connected with them and therefore images of them have appeared on many signs. It is thought that centuries ago, pub signs were used as a form of advertising and were illustrated for the benefit of those who were illiterate, a picture making the name easily distinguishable. Another purpose was to make them identifiable from other similar establishments and to promote the commodities they offered. A dog was easily recognisable and also easily depicted, as well as having many connotations throughout the ages such as companionship and loyalty, and heraldic meanings recognisable from the coats of arms of knights and noble families.[216]

Many inns were simply named the Dog, with no further explanation of the breed or role of the dog. Samuel Pepys talks of the Dog/Dogg inn at Westminster that he seemed to regularly visit to drink and dine with friends and colleagues. In 1660 he recounts his first eating of melon that year taking place at the Dog.[217] Pepys comments widely on dogs in his diaries, whether it be about the health of his own dogs, stories from foreign lands of dogs being let out at night to protect towns and cities while inhabitants slept, sporting events that included fighting dogs and even experiments carried out on them, which was common at this time.

Dogs of legend have also been popular names for inns, especially those relating to the Black Dog legend, with variations from all over the country, including its modification for *The Hound of the Baskervilles* mystery starring Sherlock Holmes. Other reasons for the name can be as simple as the proprietor owned a black, red, blue or white dog and named their establishment after their companion. In West Sussex, a pub was called the Black Dog, supposedly marking the efforts of a loyal dog to find his master, a smuggler, who was killed in the pub by revenue men.

The timorous Hare, when Started from her feat, | HARE HVNTING | with Severall Shifts, much terrour and great payne, by bloody hounds, to faue her life, soe Sweet, | | Yet dyes she by their mouths, all proves but vayne,

Hare and hounds by Wenceslas Hollar. (Wellcome Library, London)

It is local legend that the ghost of the dogs still haunts the street outside.[218] Like so many former pubs, it is now in the process of being converted to housing.[219]

Many pubs are also named after a specific breed. Historically the Talbot, a now extinct type of hunting dog, was used as a name for taverns in the medieval period.[220] Other breeds such as the greyhound and those used for hunting are often used in pub names, showing the popularity of the sport.[221]

Names such as the Dog and Bear again relate to the history of bear-baiting and the role of dogs in what was a popular pastime. The name Dog and Duck was inspired by the violent sport of duck hunting, which was popular with royalty.[222] More general links to sport and especially hunting are prominent in names such as the Fox and Hounds, Dog and Rabbit, and Dog and Gun. Pubs with these names tended to have a local connection to the sport.

There are more examples in history and the present day than can be covered here; however, from the *Dictionary of Pub Name* here are some favourites: Dog and Truck; Mad Dog; Guide Dog; and Dog and Doublet (a doublet was a garment worn by men in Tudor times and was mentioned by Shakespeare in *Julius Caesar*).[223]

Although in the current economic climate many old and new public houses have closed their doors for the final time, there are still many whose names relate to the breeds or uses of dogs.

On an online list of the most popular pub names, which is regularly updated to take into account changes of name and also those that close, there are several names that relate to dogs. Counting down, at place number 251 is Black Dog, with eighteen pubs in the UK with this name. At 229 is Dog and Gun with twenty, followed closely at 202 by Dog with twenty-three. A long gap to our next name at number 127 with forty is the Dog and Partridge. Still a popular choice, the Talbot comes in at ninety-sixth place with fifty-six and, as to be expected, the Hare and Hounds can be found at number thirty-six with a total of 130 pubs. Very close is the Fox and Hounds with 141 but the most popular dog-related pub name is Greyhound with 151 establishments and at number twenty-six on the list.[224] The highest ranked name on the list currently is the Red Lion with a staggering 590 pubs using this name in the UK.

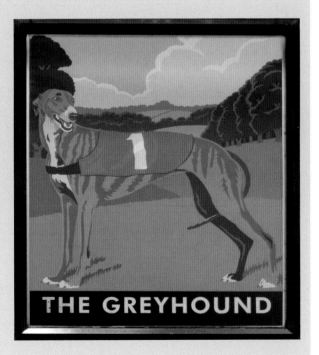

THE GREYHOUND

87 | German Shepherd

This breed is enormously popular as both working dogs and as pets. Of course, their country of origin is Germany and the story begins at the end of the nineteenth century when the breed was promoted and developed by Max von Stephanitz. He was successful in demonstrating the breed's uses to the German police and military forces and German shepherds soon became the number one choice, although the dog's original role was as a herding dog.[225]

The breed became popular in Britain after the First World War. However, it was marketed under the name Alsatian to avoid losing patronage because of its association with its homeland. By the outbreak of the Second World War, breeders in the UK were promoting German shepherds for use in the military and police forces, and many were used for these purposes during the conflict: mine detecting, searching for casualties, guard dogs, sentries and as message carriers.

A German shepherd undertaking police training. (Kachalkina Veronika)

Two of the most famous German shepherds are Strongheart and Rin Tin Tin, both American movie stars. Rin Tin Tin began his life as a German war dog who was rescued by an American, Lee Duncan, after his kennel was bombed when he was only days old.

Today the German shepherd can be seen everywhere. The dog makes a clever and loyal companion, but also works with military and police forces across the world. It is a popular choice for roles that require a great deal of training as the breed is very clever and hard-working and can be found acting as detection dogs, general-purpose police dogs, bomb and explosive detection dogs as well as in many other important roles.

A German Shepherd.
(Myers Photography)

88 | Hyde Park Cemetery

Although it is not a publically accessible area of the park, if you know where to look you can peer through the railings to see a touching cemetery of small headstones left by mourning pet owners to their beloved animals. Here the devotion and thought that the British people bequeath to their pets is extremely evident. This Victorian creation is superseded by many modern ones, which are today in high demand.

This small plot in Hyde Park is located by Victoria Lodge and was started by Mr Winbridge, the gatekeeper there. The cemetery is within the garden of the lodge itself, where many owners walked their dogs and so were well known to each other. When their pets died, Winbridge offered the owners the opportunity to lay them to rest in the park where they had enjoyed countless hours of fun. The first was a dog called Cherry, who it is believed was a Maltese, but it was not only dogs and cats who were included. Other animals, such as birds and even a monkey, are interred in Hyde Park.

Postcards were made showing sections of the cemetery with their tiny tombstones, which today are covered in moss and have grass growing around them. Some of the epitaphs bring to light the affection the Victorians had for their pets: 'Dear Little Prince'; 'Darling "Wisp" Faithful unto Death'; 'Maudie –An Old Friend'.

A Maltese like Cherry, the first dog to be buried at the park. (Degtyaryov Andrey, Shutterstock)

The names of these animals also give indications of their character, such as: Robin, Trap, Pluto, Butcha, Floss, Ponto, Tippo and Bobbie. The Internet furnishes many images of the cemetery, so it is easy to glimpse some of the tiny tombstones with their names and epitaphs. The last burial took place in 1903 and the plot is filled with around 300 burials.

In the course of this book we will look at other cemeteries that demonstrate the care and loyalty that human owners gave to their pets when they died. The important role that these dogs played as family members is clear from the fact that they were laid to rest in the same sensitive way that a human relative would be.[226]

Vintage postcard of the cemetery. (The History Press)

The Dog's Cemetery, Hyde Park, London.

89 | Sandringham Estate

Set in the beautiful Norfolk countryside, Sandringham House has been the retreat of British monarchs since 1862. The connection with dogs at the estate is clear, as the Sandringham kennels were established there in 1879 and built to house 100 dogs. The breeding at the kennels has been very successful under Queen Elizabeth II, with five show champions from the estate. The queen names all of the puppies born at the kennels and all are registered with the prefix 'Sandringham' with The Kennel Club.[227]

Below: Memorial stones at Sandringham. (Sandringham Estate)

Right: An early fifteenth-century illustrated treatise on the Church showing Christ sitting in the doorway of a church with a small dog. (Wellcome Library, London)

Some of the cherished royal pets are also lovingly remembered in touching memorial stones in the gardens of Sandringham House. There are three stones which commemorate three of the queen's dogs and all record name, date of birth and death as well as 'The Faithful Companion of the Queen'.

One of the stones is to Susan, a corgi given to the queen on her 18th birthday by her father, and must therefore have been very special to her. It is from Susan that the other corgis were bred.

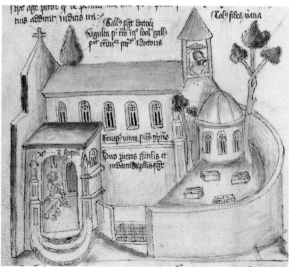

90 | Jack Russell

The Jack Russell only become recognised as pedigreed by The Kennel Club in 2015. New breeds are not often recognised by The Kennel Club, with only six new ones incorporated since 2008.[228] Previously the breed had been known as a 'type' of terrier in order to cover the variation of fox terriers known as Jack Russells, which are very popular and can always be found enjoying local open spaces with its usually happy and energetic nature.

Terrier comes from the Latin *terra*, which means earth, and can be traced to the terrier group's history of hunting the fox and badger into their underground homes. Both smooth and wired type of the Jack Russell terrier, also known as the Parson Jack Russell terrier, have their beginnings in the fox terrier breed. This variety of fox terrier has a long history, starting with its breeding by a Victorian parson, Revd John Russell, who bred them as hunting dogs and also bestowed his name on them.

Jack Russell. (Mary Evans Picture Library)

Despite its only recent pedigree status, the Jack Russell has long been a favourite for both hunting and as a pet. This breed is also popular with royalty: the Duchess of Cornwall owns two called Rosie and Tosca.

The breed found further fame in the film *The Artist* (2011), a black-and-white silent movie. The film was critically acclaimed winning five Oscars, three Golden Globes and six BAFTAs, including Best Actor, Best Film and Best Original Screenplay.[229] In *The Artist* a Jack Russell fetches a policeman to save his master from a deadly fire; this character was played by a dog called Uggie, who had already appeared in *Water for Elephants* (2011). Uggie walked the red carpet at *The Artist* film premier, had a promotional tour which included *The Graham Norton Show* in the UK and was so popular that a book was published about him in 2012. Sadly he was put to sleep in August 2015 at the age of 13 after developing prostate cancer.

91 | K-9

With all the discussion of real dogs, it is important to acknowledge the part that created dogs play in our history, imagination, and entertainment ... even when they are not technically flesh and blood.

K-9 is a dog whose reinvention continues through the Doctor Who series and its spin offs. A canine companion for time travel adventure, K-9 was built to last and is clever, capable of independent thought and equipped with a laser. At tricky moments in the plot, K-9 would often appear as a *deus ex machina* to save the Doctor and his companions. His first appearance was in the 1977 series with Tom Baker as the Doctor and, although he has been remodelled since his first appearance, he has continued to pop up over the course of the Doctor Who franchise. Since then he has appeared in the spin off *The Sarah Jane Adventures*, as well as his own series in 2010 where he had an overhaul, becoming a more modern version of himself for a new audience.

K-9 at the Dr Who exhibition in Cardiff 2010. (williamsdb/flikr)

92 | Kemberton

In the quiet village of Kemberton near Shifnal, Shropshire lies the beautiful church of St John the Baptist and St Andrew. Apart from being a beautiful rural church, inside a set of tiles can be found on the floor by the altar.

The church has been renovated and rebuilt no fewer than six times and in 1780, during one renovation, the remains of a thirteenth-century church were found. In the last renovation some tiles were uncovered. Very little is known about these tiles, other than they were originally made in Wales and depict three hunting scenes:

A man blowing a horn
Three hounds in chase
A stag and dogs

Tile depicting stag and hound, Kemberton. (Emma White)

Craven Dunhill of Jackfield recreated the tiles that can be seen in the church today (the originals were taken away to be rehomed in a more suitable place for conservation). However, only two of the scenes, those depicting the man blowing a horn and the stag and dogs, were reproduced.

These tiles serve as a wonderful reminder of the value of dogs in the lives of past centuries but also of the status they provided. Tiles such of these were likely to depict those landowners and gentry with the wealth to own such animals, and using them as decoration within the local church would have been a status symbol.[230]

93 | Old English Sheepdog

The Old English sheepdog is known, rightly or wrongly, by children and adults alike as the Dulux Dog. Although some would say this hasn't helped the breed, it has made it known to a nation of people who might otherwise, without living in the countryside, have never seen one. The first use of the dog in Dulux advertising was in 1961 and the breed has become synonymous with the brand ever since.

Opposite: Old English sheepdog. (Bikeriderlondon, Shutterstock)

Below: Old English bobtails in the snow. (Olga_i, Shutterstock)

This is a dog that is perceived as having a British origin; however, it is thought to have originally derived from European shepherd dogs such as the Bergamasco, whose coat, although not the same as the Old English sheepdog, is similar.[231] However, the Old English sheepdog is also thought to be more of a drover's dog than a sheepdog in the tradition sense of herding sheep. The breed is also sometimes referred to as the 'bobtail' because of its docked tail. Historically, owners of sheepdogs with docked tails were exempt from paying duty, the consequences of which meant that many dogs had their tails docked.[232]

This breed is easily recognisable from its coat and it is a dog only for those with the patience and time for such a beautifully wild coat. Perhaps this is the reason that they are currently on the At Watch list of native breeds with The Kennel Club, who are monitoring registration of Old English Sheepdog puppies as numbers of registrations on average have barely gone over 400 since 2011.[233]

94 | Bothie

Sir Ranulph Fiennes is known as the foremost British explorer of his time, a reputation that will no doubt continue for generations to come. His achievements include being the first person to visit both the North and South Poles, climbing Mount Everest, completing the Land Rover '7 marathons 7 continents 7 days' Challenge in 2003 and many more. He has also written widely on the subject of exploration and discovery.

An engraving showing a dog sledge of the British Arctic expedition of 1875–76. (©Illustrated London News Ltd/Mary Evans Picture Library)

The subject of interest here, however, is the Transglobe expedition that he and his team completed between 1979 and 1982. The aim of the expedition was to travel the world vertically from pole to pole using only surface transport.

One companion on this trip was Ranulph and his wife Virginia's pet terrier called Bothie. Although Bothie couldn't take part in the whole trip owing to the risk of him catching diseases in certain areas, he was brought in for the routes covered by boat and also at both the North and South Poles.[234] In the Antarctic he was clothed in boots and a body stocking in order to keep him warm in the freezing temperatures.

Bothie's adventures were published in a book written by Virginia and Ranulph called *Bothie the Polar Dog*, and he was extremely popular with the public. He even made a lap of the ring at Crufts in 1983 to mark his wonderful achievements.

While Bothie was on his expedition he met a black Newfoundland Labrador cross called Blackdog in Canada. The two became inseparable and Blackdog returned home with Fiennes.

Bothie is not the first dog to explore the polar regions. In the summer of 1875 the British Admiralty sent Captain George Nares with two ships, HMS *Alert* and HMS *Discovery*, to make an attempt to reach the North Pole via Smith Sound. Although the attempt was unsuccessful, a new furthest north record was set, the coasts of Greenland and Ellesmere Island were charted and much scientific data was gathered. When the two ships spent the winter frozen in separate bays, dogs were used to pull sledges between the two.

Engraving showing the dog Ginger attempting to board the Arctic expedition of 1875–76 (©Illustrated London News Ltd/Mary Evans Picture Library)

95 | North Tuddenham

In a small Norfolk village, an unusual window can be found in the porch of the parish church. While the occupant of the section of stained glass is unusual, its place is not high up to be gazed upon but is rather at touchable level. It is not original to the church but rather an addition by a nineteenth-century vicar who sourced the glass, which is believed to be medieval.

Relatively little is known about the glass, but what is important is the scene it depicts, showing the importance of dogs in medieval society. It shows two dogs with the appearance of greyhounds, with fine gold or brass collars and leads. These may have been sight hounds depicted as part of a hunting scene, but it will probably never be known exactly what the large scene portrayed or indeed where the original home of the glass was.

Unfortunately, the section of the stained-glass window depicting the dogs has recently been damaged and is waiting for funds to be raised to cover the cost of the delicate repair work.

Left: North Tuddenham group
(Phil Hewitt)

Opposite: Stained-glass
window at North Tuddenham
(Phil Hewitt)

96 | Religious Dogs

Often it is the anecdotal tales that endear animals to us. They may not have been empirically proven or grounded in fact, but these are usually the stories we do remember and pass on to others. The cynical among us may show displeasure at the inclusion of such tales; however, while the whole story may not be strictly verifiable, there is often truth at its core. Moreover, these stories often have the effect of reminding us of the characteristics of our own pets.

George R. Jesse's *Researches into the History of the British Dog* is full of enigmatic and humbling anecdotes about dogs, and the two regarding canines with a penchant for religious services are well worth repeating 150 years after the book's publication. Jesse anonymised his sources for both stories; however, this does not detract from the human characteristics that both dogs display.

The first tale concerns a Newfoundland, 'who rendered himself quite notorious in the neighbourhood from the regularity with which he attended the funerals. No sooner did the procession appear on the road leading to the church than the dog darted off at full speed. Having joined it he composed his demeanour, walked quietly up and took his place as chief mourner immediately after the coffin, and so accompanied it to the place of interment; thence returning quickly home when the ceremony was over.'[235]

The second story involves a large bloodhound, whose owner was a vicar, and who had acquired the habit of going to church with the family:

He always behaved with the greatest decorum, lying at the foot of the pulpit stairs, till one unfortunate day, when a stranger officiated in lieu of his master. The dog seemed to take no notice until the communion service; but when the stranger was within the altar rails and had just commenced the reading of the first commandment, then the dog uprose, placed his fore paws on the rails, and gave utterance to a fearful bay. The stranger, being of timid temperament, fled to the vestry room, and the hound was ignominiously expelled, and for some time was kept chained up on Sundays during service.

The story, however, was not finished, and after a while the dog was no longer restrained on Sundays, and he no longer attempted to enter the church. Jesse concludes that the dog began absenting himself on Sundays. No one knew where he went, or very much cared as he always returned afterwards, until one of the vicar's daughters was stopped in the street by an angry woman:

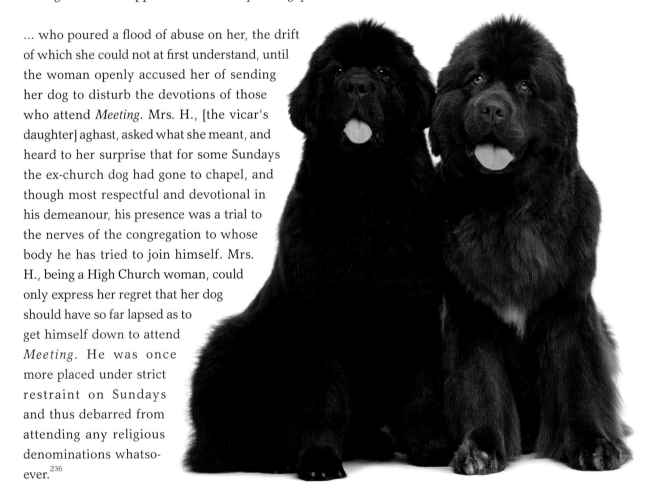

Newfoundland puppies. One Victorian Newfoundland gained a strange reputation for attending funerals ... (Eric Isselee, Shutterstock)

... who poured a flood of abuse on her, the drift of which she could not at first understand, until the woman openly accused her of sending her dog to disturb the devotions of those who attend *Meeting*. Mrs. H., [the vicar's daughter] aghast, asked what she meant, and heard to her surprise that for some Sundays the ex-church dog had gone to chapel, and though most respectful and devotional in his demeanour, his presence was a trial to the nerves of the congregation to whose body he has tried to join himself. Mrs. H., being a High Church woman, could only express her regret that her dog should have so far lapsed as to get himself down to attend *Meeting*. He was once more placed under strict restraint on Sundays and thus debarred from attending any religious denominations whatso-ever.[236]

97 | Search and Rescue

Leisure pursuits such as walking, hiking and mountaineering can lead us into dangerous or inhospitable places. The brave men and women, often volunteers, who are dispatched to find us if we get into difficulty are often accompanied by our canine friends for their expertise and their noses. Dogs have millions more scent receptors in their noses than humans and more of their brain is dedicated to working out these smells than our own. Therefore their ability to track humans, either via the ground we have walked over or by the aromas we give off into the air, is exceptional, making them ideal for the job.

Opposite: St Bernards attempting to revive and rescue a victim. (Wellcome Library, London)

Below: Convent of Great St Bernard in 1837. (Wellcome Library, London)

These dogs, like those specialised animals in police forces and the armed services, are highly trained to carry out their task. Many breeds are used for this work today, with lowland and mountain rescue organisations operating throughout the UK.

However, the original rescue dog is the St Bernard, which became the saviour of many a lost traveller on the Great St Bernard Pass in the mountains between Switzerland and Italy. The name of the breed derives from the monk who set up the hospice for travellers crossing the treacherous mountains. These dogs would go out into the snow-covered terrain, looking for travellers who may have lost their way in blizzards and avalanches. It is speculated that they would carry a small barrel on their collars that was filled with brandy. However, it is more likely this was added to images of the dogs for artistic effect.

Training a dog to work as
a rescue team. (Wellcome
Library, London)

Opposite: Modern St Bernard
with rescue keg. (Fedor
Selivanov, Shutterstock)

Today the work of those early dogs and the first-aid dogs that followed is continued through the modern search and rescue services.

98 | The Dog Who Saved the World Cup

The year 1966 is significant in many people's minds due to England hosting and winning the football World Cup. The prize at this time was the gold Jules Rimet cup and the celebrations after England's 4–2 victory over West Germany may have been remembered differently had the queen not actually handed the cup to the team after the game. However, this was a distinct possibility, as the cup had been stolen months before the final. Luckily for the Football Association (FA) a plucky canine located the trophy a week later.

Pickles posing near the spot where he found the trophy, in Beulah Hill, Norwood, South London. (Central Press/Getty Images)

The background to the story was that, after arriving in England in January 1966, the cup was kept safe by the FA. They would allow the trophy to be displayed at events but normally for no more than a few hours. However, in March the FA agreed to have the trophy displayed at a stamp exhibition in London over several days. They stipulated that there was to be a security guard next to a glass case that housed the trophy at all times, even when the exhibit was closed, plus other guards in the building. The trophy was insured for £30,000.

On 20 March 1966, a Sunday, the exhibit was closed to the public but the ground floor of the exhibition hall was a Methodist church and therefore open for the service and also a Sunday School. The guard who was supposed to be guarding the case at all times was, in fact, only hired to be there when the exhibition was open to the public, therefore contravening the FA's conditions. Thieves broke into the building via the back entrance and took the trophy from its glass case sometime between 11 a.m. and 12 p.m.

After the theft, the chairman of the FA received a note and a parcel containing the top of the trophy; the rest of it was being held ransom for £15,000.[237] After a failed police operation to get the trophy from the thieves, it was still no closer to being found.

A week after the trophy was stolen, a Thames waterman named David Corbett left his house on Beulah Hill, South Norwood to make a telephone call across the road and took his 1-year-old dog, Pickles, with him. Pickles was very interested in a parked car and the hedge which ran alongside it and he continued to sniff it. His owner decided to investigate and found an object wrapped in newspaper and tied with string. On further inspection he discovered it was the Jules Rimet cup and, after recovering from the shock of what he had found, headed to a police station to hand it in.

David and Pickles became overnight celebrities, pushing Prime Minister Harold Wilson off the front cover of the newspapers during the run up to a general election. Pictures of Pickles appeared in newspapers next to the story. He was named 'Dog of the Year' and was awarded a silver medal by the National Canine Defence League (now Dog's Trust). Pickles even went on to star in a film called *The Spy with the Cold Nose*. He also received a year's worth of dog food and his owners received around £6,000 in reward money.[238] However, not a penny of that came from the FA. Pickles and Corbett were invited to the England team's dinner after they won the World Cup, where Pickles was made a fuss of.

Sadly, the black-and-white mongrel who saved England from the embarrassment of having lost the Jules Rimet cup died only six months later after getting his lead caught on a fallen tree while chasing a cat. His owner buried him in the garden of his house, bought with part of the reward money.

The story of Pickles finding the World Cup is revived every four years when the World Cup comes around. And, with the next World Cup being in Brazil, where the cup was stolen again, it is even more likely that the story of Pickles will be pawed over again!

The World Cup did not stay found. In 1983 the real cup was given to Brazil to keep in recognition of their achievement in winning the cup three times, after their victory in 1970. But it was stolen and has never been seen again.

99 | A Puppy Rescue

Most of us will hopefully never have to see the animal protection legislation Britain has enacted put into force, but it is there to give charities the power to step in when animals are at risk. One way this is carried out is by RSPCA inspectors, who respond to calls of concern in the community.

In early 2009 a horrendous case was brought to the attention of the media after an RSPCA inspection found fifteen puppies in locked suitcases in a cupboard. Cries could be heard by inspectors who, on searching the property, found the puppies, some of them less than a week old. The mothers of the puppies were also rescued.

Some of them had already succumbed to starvation, dehydration or suffocation but the survivors were taken into the care of the charity. The animals were taken to RSPCA kennels in Sussex where they were cared for by attentive staff who also reunited them with their mothers. The court case against the owner took months to make its way through the legal system and was only finalised towards the end of 2009. In the meantime, the dogs and puppies were named by the staff at the centre:

The mums of the pups were named Flo & Beth; another adult dog who was rescue was called Patch; the puppies were named: Dudie Duncan; Upsie Daisy; Iggle Piggle; Little Maff; Miss Ginnie; Macca Pacca and Antonio.

Some of the names are after characters from the children's TV show *In the Night Garden*.

Following the case, the owner of all the animals, including a cat and several other adult dogs that were also rescued, was jailed for twenty weeks and banned from owning animals in the future. After this, the RSPCA were given the legal right to begin rehoming the puppies with loving families. Many of them were renamed by their new owners. The two mums, Beth and Flo, were even found a home where they could live together.

The case was featured on the national TV programme *Dog Rescuers* on Channel 5, which highlighted the story and showed the shocking video footage of how the animals were found. It also told the story of Megan, one of the puppies who had been rehomed and renamed.

Some of the dogs and their owners kept in touch and a reunion was planned for April 2011, just over two years after their discovery. At the reunion, at least five of the puppies, their mums and some of the adult dogs that were rescued, including Patch, were brought together for the first time since they had been rehomed. There was coverage by local TV news and the press. The reunion is recounted in the newsletter of the shelter in which most of the animals were cared for, aptly called the *Newshound*. It stated that 'it was obvious that mums Beth and Flo were delighted to see their now adult puppies, and the "puppies" themselves all wanted to play with each other'.[239] They were also joined by the RSPCA inspector who had been with the team who discovered them.

One of the 'puppies', called Dudie, even has his own section in the *Newshound* that describes what's been going on in his life. Included are meetings with the local mayor, taking part in dog shows, exploring the South Downs, making lots of new friends and even going camping for the first time.[240] It really is a dog's life!

This case shows the importance of having legislation that can be enforced, as well as highlighting the vital work of those who go in to defend these defenceless animals when they need our help. There are many hundreds of cases that continue to be fought by the RSPCA and other charities to make sure that man's best friend is treated with the respect and care that he deserves.

Reunion of the dogs who were rescued from the property in East Sussex. (Private collection)

100 | Vulnerable Native Breeds

In 2003 The Kennel Club began a program that would identify any native breeds of British origin that were vulnerable to becoming extinct, as well as a list of At Watch breeds that are under observation.

The way in which The Kennel Club is able to decide on the most endangered breeds is by the number of registrations of each breed made with the club each year. To be considered vulnerable, the breed has to have had fewer that 300 registrations made in a year. To be put on the At Watch list, the number of registrations must be fewer than 500.

Some of the breeds are surprising for their inclusion, as they are easily recognisable to even the uneducated eye; however, as taste in dogs as well as their working roles have changed and declined, previously strong breeds are beginning to struggle. A few of those that are deemed vulnerable are:

Bloodhound, which has failed to reach 100 registrations a year since 2010. In four out of the last five years for which figures are available, numbers haven't broken out of the fifties.

King Charles spaniel, though not as much as the bloodhound, with registrations around the 150–200 mark.

Mastiff, one of the oldest breeds of the country, the registration numbers not breaking 180 in the last five counts.

A number of spaniel breeds, including the Irish water, field, clumber and Sussex.

English setter in light colours. (Erik Lam, Shutterstock)

The At Watch list includes some favourites such as the English Setter and the Old English Sheepdog. Registrations for these two breeds are in the 300s and 400s on average respectively.[241]

It is very sad to think of any breed of dog becoming extinct, especially as some of those that are in danger have a long and illustrious history in Britain. Just as we conserve documents for historical record, so too should these breeds be given the conservation and preservation that their long and devoted service to our countries deserves.

English setter in dark colours. (Alexey Stiop, Shutterstock)

Conclusion

Writing this book has been a challenge, but also a revelation. As a child I had very little contact with dogs and had one bad experience as a teenager, which made me feel anxious around them; I was mainly affectionate, therefore, with cats. However, in my early twenties my family was joined by a rescue puppy from Foal Farm, near Biggin Hill, Kent, and my whole perception was changed.

Saxon had been abandoned along with the rest of his litter on Streatham Common and was at the centre to be rehomed. He was so lively and clever when we first met him that, even with my apprehension of dogs, it would have been impossible not to want to give him a new home.

He grew with our family and today is just as special, if not more so, since I have left home as I see him much less. He is always excited to see any of us and fill us with laughter at his silly behaviour; he is a constant reminder of how wonderful a life shared with a dog can be. Saxon can always be found with a smile and a listening ear, and I would not wish for a life without him. That is why this book is dedicated to him.

I hope that the stories that fill these pages add a little historical understanding to some of the origins and uses of dogs, as well as their continuing role in our modern lives. Whether we own a dog or not, they still protect us in the police forces, aid the military as search dogs and, of course, provide hours of entertainments as puppets and cartoons on TV.

Major Richardson, or Lieutenant Colonel as he became by the end of the Second World War, has been mentioned many times in this book, and not without reason. In his final book, *Fifty Years with Dogs*, written together with his wife and published after his death in 1948, they wrote a stirring passage to finish the story of their work before and after two world wars. Their words still have resonance today and mirror my own thoughts and, therefore, for Richardson and the millions of dogs humans have known:

We have come to the end of our tale. It has been a joy to write it and we fervently trust we have conveyed a sense of comfort and hope which can be derived from the happy association with the animal world, especially of dogs, in the daily work of life. There is so much that is drab or monotonous in day-to-day life, but this can be inspired with joy, humour, and amusement by the affection and happiness expressed towards us by our canine friends. We are indeed grateful for this. We send our greetings to all those friends from overseas and elsewhere who have visited us to obtain protection and companionship from the numerous Jacks, Jocks, Bessies, Bennys, and Bellas who have gone forth from our kennels with a good job of work to do – in new homes near and far away.

Hail and Farewell[242]

About the Author

Emma White has a Masters degree from the University of Birmingham in First World War studies and is now studying for a PhD at the University of Chichester in the military employment of dogs during the conflict. She was previously project manager for West Sussex County Council (WSCC) Library Service's 'Great War: West Sussex' project. The book resulting from the project won the Alan Ball Local History Award from the Chartered Institute of Library and Information Professionals. Emma is currently managing the 'Military Voices Past & Present' project for WSCC Library Service.

Also by the Author
Great War Britain: West Sussex Remembering 1914–18 (The History Press, 2014)

Saxon

Endnotes

1   S. Jones, *Exploring the World of the Celts* (London: Thames and Hudson Ltd, 1993), p.54

2   Stabo, *The Geography of Strabo: Book IV Chapter V*, translated by H.C. Hamilton & W. Falconer, (London: Henry G. Bohn, 1854), p.291

3   C. Reeves, *Pleasures & Pastimes in Medieval England* (Stroud: Alan Sutton Publishing Limited, 1995), pp.107–8

4   www.bayeuxmuseum.com/en/la_tapisserie_de_bayeux_en.html (accessed 25/08/2015)

5   E. Carson Paston and S.D. White with K. Gilbert, *The Bayeux Tapestry and Its Contexts: A Reassessment* (Woodridge: The Boydell Press, 2014), p.73

6   E. Hallam, *Domesday Souvenir Guide* (Richmond: Public Record Office, 2000), p.3

7   John S. More, *Domesday Book: Gloucestershire*, general editor John Morris (Chichester: Phillimore, 1982) Introduction

8   Hallam, *Domesday Souvenir Guide*, p.7

9   More, *Domesday Book*, Introduction

10 More, *Domesday Book*, Chapter 1: Land of the King, Section 1 (162d)

11 J. Winters, 'Forest Law' on Early English Laws: www.earlyenglishlaws.ac.uk/reference/essays/forest-law/ (accessed 06/02/2016)

12 J. Manwood, *Treatise of the Forest Laws: Enlarged and corrected by W. Nelson* (London: C. Nutt, 1717 (1598)), pp.107–9

13 Ibid., p.116

14 Ibid., p.123

15 Ibid., pp.117–8

16 The National Archives Currency Converter www.nationalarchives.gov.uk/currency/default0.asp#mid (accessed 06/02/2016)

17 Manwood, *Treatise of the Forest Laws*, p.110

18 www.finerollshenry3.org.uk/home.html (accessed 01/02/2016)

19 Roll of fines from the seventh year of King Henry son of King John, 7 Henry III (28 October 1222– 27 October 1223), Fine Roll C 60/18: Membrane 9 No 35 www.finerollshenry3.org.uk/content/calendar/roll_018.html (accessed 01/02/2016)

20 Rolls of fines from the sixteenth year of King Henry son of King John: 16 Henry III (29 October 1226–27 October 1232), Fine Roll C 60/31: Membrane 5 No 114

21 Reeves, *Pleasures & Pastimes in Medieval England*, p.103

22 Ibid., p.105

23 *Edward, Duke of York, The Master of Game*, edited by W.A. & F. Baillie-Grohman (London: Chatto & Windus, 1909 (c.1420)), pp.5–7

24 Ibid., p.9

25 Ibid., p.22

26 E.E. Power, *Medieval English Nunneries c. 1275–1535*, (Cambridge: Cambridge University Press, 1922), p.305

27 Power, *Medieval English Nunneries c. 1275-1535*, p.306

28 Victoria County History, 'Houses of the Cistercians nuns; Priory of Keldholme' in *A History of the County of York: Volume 3*: (London: Victoria County History, 1974) pp.167–9.

29 Ibid.

30 Victoria County History, 'Houses of the Cistercians nuns; Rosedale Priory' in *A History of the County of*

Jackson

Maggie

York: Volume 3: (London: Victoria County History, 1974) pp.174–5.

31 G. Chaucer, *The Canterbury Tales: Translated by Nevill Coghill Volume I* (London: The Folio Society, 1956), p.14

32 Ibid., pp.20–1

33 Ibid., pp.21–2

34 National Trust, *Lyme Park: House and Garden* (Great Britain: National Trust, 1998), p.27

35 S. Slater, *The Illustrated Book of Heraldry: An International History of Heraldry and its Contemporary Uses* (London: Hermes House, 2006 (2002))

36 Annual Register, or a View of the History, Politics and Literature, for the Year 1789 (London: 1792), pp.223–4

37 The Aldine, Vol. 5 (The Aldine Press, 1872) p.60.

38 Annual Register, or a View of the History, Politics and Literature, for the Year 1789, pp.223–4

39 Edward, Duke of York, *The Master of Game*, p.113

40 Ibid., p.115

41 H. Dalziel, *British Dogs: Their Varieties, History, Characteristics, Breeding, Management and Exhibition* (London: 'The Bazaar' Office, c. 1880), p.14

42 E. Topsel, *The History of Four-footed Beasts and Serpents* (London, 1655), p.114

43 Dalziel, *British Dogs*, p.20

44 J. Caius, *Of Englishe Dogges, the diversities, the names, the natures, and the* properties (1570) translated into English by Abraham Fleming (London: Richard Johnes, 1576 (1881)), p.10

45 Ibid., pp.34–5

46 T. Bewick, *A General History of Quadrupeds* (Newcastle Upon Tyne: S. Hodgson, R. Beilby, and T. Bewick, 1800), p.365

47 E. Jesse, *Anecdotes of Dogs* (London: Henry G. Bohn, 1858), pp.418–20

48 *The Kennel Club's Illustrated Breed Standards: The Official Guide to Registered Breeds* (London: Ebury Press, 1998), pp.106–10.

49 A. Weir, *Henry VIII: King & Court* (London, 2008), p.31; Tudor Britain online learning resources www.tudorbritain.org (pdf accessed 12/11/2014)

50 Weir, *Henry VIII*, p.31

51 'Henry VIII: Privy Purse Expenses', *Letters and Papers, Foreign and Domestic, Henry VIII, Volume 5: 1531–1532* (1800), 11 May 1530, pp.747–62

52 'Henry VIII: Privy Purse Expenses', *Volume 5: 1531–1532*, 14 May 1530

53 'Henry VIII: Privy Purse Expenses', *Volume 5: 1531–1532*, 2 February 1531

54 The National Archives currency converter http://apps.nationalarchives.gov.uk/currency/results.asp#mid (accessed 14/11/2014). Note the 'today' prices are for 2005

55 Weir, *Henry VIII*, p.31 (original to be found within 'Inventories of the Wardrobe of King Henry VIII')

56 Letter from Sir Frances Bryan to Lord Lisle 'Henry VIII: January 1534, 16–20', *Letters and Papers, Foreign and Domestic, Henry* VIII, Volume 7: 1534 (1883), 20 January 1534, pp.30–6

57 National Portrait Gallery www.npg.org.uk/learning/digital/portraiture/perspective-seeing-where-you-stand/drawing.php (accessed 14/11/2014)

58 K. MacDonogh, *Reigning Cats and Dogs: A History of Pets at Court since the Renaissance* (Fourth Estate Limited, 1999), pp.78–9

59 C. Skidmore, *Edward VI: The Lost King of England* (Weidenfeld & Nicolson, 2007), p.103

60 Skidmore, *Edward VI*, p.105

61 Mary Rose Museum www.maryrose.org/ (accessed 14/11/2014)

62 Mary Rose Museum www.maryrose.org/discover-our-collection/story-of-the-ship/henry-viii-the-mary-rose/ (accessed 14/11/2014)

63 Mary Rose Museum www.maryrose.org/discover-our-collection/her-crew/life-on-board/ (accessed 14/11/2014)

64 Mary Rose Museum www.maryrose.org/identifying-the-mary-rose-dog/ (accessed 14/11/2014)

65 Mary Rose Museum www.maryrose.org/identifying-the-mary-rose-dog/ (accessed 14/11/2014)

66 M. Ashley, *A Brief History of British Kings and Queens* (London, Robinson Publishing, 1998), p.253

67 Ashley, *A Brief History of British Kings and Queens*, p.297

68 MacDonogh, *Reigning Cats and Dogs*, p.46

69 Shakespeare: The British Library, www.bl.uk/treasures/shakespeare/basics.html (accessed 03/02/2016)

70 S. Coren, *The Pawprints of History: Dogs and the Course of Human Events* (New York: Free Press, 2003), pp.256–7

71 Ibid., p.257

72 Ibid., p.257

73 A. Croxton Smith, 'Dog in Literature' in *The Book of the Dog* (London: Nicholson & Watson, 1948) p.899

74 J. Lockhart, *Lockhart's Life of Scott*, abridged by O. Leon Reid (New York: The Macmillan Company, 1914), pp.193–4

75 Ibid., p.76

76 Croxton Smith, 'Dog in Literature' in *The Book of the Dog*, p.900

77 Ibid., pp.900–1

78 T. Moore, *Life of Byron: with his letters and journals: Volume 1* (London: John Murray, 1854), p.135

79 Ibid., pp.221–2

80 Ibid., p.222

81 George R. Jesse, *Researches into the History of the British Dog, from Ancient Laws, Charters and Historical Records: Volume 1* (London: Robert Hardwick, 1866) p.25

82 J. Caius, *Of Englishe Dogges, the diversities, the names, the natures, and the properties*, p.25

83 T. Bewick, *A General History of Quadrupeds*, p.334

84 W. Wordsworth, *Poems in Two Volumes: Volume Two* (London: Longman, Hurst, Rees, and Orme, 1807), pp.99–101

85 Ibid.

86 Information from a conversation with Nigel Crompton of the Historical Branch (Fire Service)

87 *The Morning Post* (London, England) 29 March 1834 and 16 October 1835

88 'Chance, The Firemen's Dog' in *Sussex Advertiser*, 21 December 1835, p.4

89 Ibid., p.4

90 Coren, *The Pawprints of History*, p.12

91 Ibid., pp.12–3

92 Ibid., p.13

93 H. Mayhew, *London Labour and the London Poor: Volume 4* (London: Griffin, Bohn and Company, 1862), p.326.

94 'A Spaniel Dog' in *The Times*, Issue 461, Wednesday, 14 June 1786, p.3

95 Printed notice about a dog stolen at Chichester from Peckham Williams, 3 March 1745. The Goodwood Estate Archives MSS 46, West Sussex Record Office. Courtesy of the Trustees of the Goodwood Collection

96 D. Beevers, *Preston Manor: Brighton* (Royal Pavilion, Libraries & Museums, 1999), p.32

97 Ibid., p.5

98 M. Roberts, 'The Companionship of Dogs: Happy Lives at Preston Manor' in *Sussex Daily News*, Tuesday, 26 March 1935

99 'The Murders in London' in *The Times*, Issue 32522, Saturday, 20 October 1888, p.7

100 'Bloodhounds and the Police' in *The Times*, Issue 46867, Monday, 24 September 1934, p.18

101 The British Monarchy: Royal Animals www.royal.gov.uk/TheRoyalHousehold/RoyalAnimals/Familypets.aspx (accessed 06/02/2016)

Monty

102 Jesse, *Researches into the History of the British Dog, from Ancient Laws, Charters and Historical Records*, p.166

103 Ibid., p.166

104 H. Mayhew, Vol 3, 'The Dancing Dogs', p.181

105 Ibid., p.182

106 Theatre Royal, Perth, *Perthshire Courier*, 7 September 1837, p.2

107 Mayhew, Vol. 1, Preface

108 Ibid, Preface

109 Ibid, p.358

110 Bank of England Inflation Calculator www.bankofengland.co.uk/education/Pages/resources/inflationtools/calculator/flash/default.aspx

111 www.thekennelclub.org.uk/our-resources/about-the-kennel-club/history-of-the-kennel-club/ (accessed 01/12/2015)

112 A. Croxton Smith, 'How the Kennel World is Governed', in *The Book of the Dog*, edited by B. Vasey-Fitzgerald (London: Nicholson & Watson, 1948), pp.813

113 'Accident To A Famous Railway Dog' in *Sheffield Daily Telegraph*, 17 January 1882, p.3

114 'A Famous Dog' in *York Herald*, 1 November 1890, p.15

115 'Death Of A Famous Dog' in *Exeter and Plymouth Gazette*, 15 December 1891, p.8

116 S. Stall, *100 Dogs Who Changed Civilization: History's Most Influential Canines* (Philadelphia: Quirk Books, 2007), p.118

117 Mayhew, Vol 3, 'Jimmy Shaw' p.9

118 Ibid., pp.9–10

119 'The Rat-Worrying Match' in *Windsor and Eton Express*, 1 August 1829, p.1

120 'Official Rat-Catcher's Loss' in *Folkestone, Hythe, Sandgate and Cheriton Herald*, 1 May 1926, p.9

121 M. Swash and D. Millar, *Airedale Terriers* (Wiltshire: The Crowood Press Ltd, 1991), p.9

122 Dalziel, *British Dogs*, pp.173–4

123 R. Colville, 'A History of Cruft's Dog Show' in *The Book of the Dog*, pp.843–5

124 www.crufts.org.uk/content/show-information/history-of-crufts/ (accessed 01/12/2015)

125 Colville, 'A History of Cruft's Dog Show' in *The Book of the Dog*, pp.850

126 B. Cummins, *Colonel Richardson's Airedales: The Making of the British War Dog School 1900–1918*, (Calgary, Detselig Enterprises Ltd., 2003), pp.86–7

127 Ibid., p.87

Ginny, Maggie and Tia

128 Metropolitan Police Force: Dog Support Unit, http://content.met.police.uk/Article/Who-are-we-and-what-do-we-do/1400010412153/1400010412153 (accessed 07/02/2016)

129 'Famous Dog "Retires"' in *Sheffield Evening Telegraph*, 22 March 1913, p.4

130 'Bedfordshire's oldest police drug dog to retire this weekend' in *Bedfordshire on Sunday*, 18 January 2016, www.bedfordshire-news.co.uk/Bedfordshire-s-oldest-police-drug-dog-retire/story-28548976-detail/story.html (accessed 07/02/2016)

131 D. Lynch, *Titanic: An Illustrated History*, (London, Hodder & Stoughton, 1996 (1992)), p.100

132 Ibid.

133 R. Davenport-Hines, *Titanic Lives: Migrants and Millionaires, Conmen and Crew* (London, HarperPress, 2012), p.164

134 Ibid., pp.173–4

135 J. Eaton and C. Haas, *Titanic: A Journey Through Time* (Wellingborough: Patrick Stephens Limited, 1999), p.234

136 Davenport-Hines, *Titanic Lives*, p.174

137 Eaton and Haas, *Titanic: A Journey Through Time*, p.234

138 Davenport-Hines, *Titanic Lives*, p.348

139 History of the international guide dog movement from Guide Dogs for the Blind, www.guidedogs.org.uk/

abscutus/guide-dogs-organisation/history#.VrZu-DbcuP8 (accessed 06/02/2016)

140 N. Liakoff, 'Guide Dogs for the Blind', in *The Book of the Dog*, p.939

141 Ibid., pp.949–50

142 Guide Dogs for the Blind: National Breeding Centre, www.guidedogs.org.uk/aboutus/national-breeding-centre#.VrZu3jbcuP8 (accessed 06/02/2016)

143 E. H. Richardson, *War, Police and Watch Dogs* (London: William Blackwood and Sons, 1910), p.38

144 E. H. Richardson, *Fifty Years with Dogs* (London: Hutchinson & Co, 1950), p.37

145 E. H. Richardson, *Forty Years with Dogs* (London: Hutchinson & Co, 1929), p.113–4

146 E. H. Richardson, *Watch Dogs: Their Training and Management* (London, Hutchinson & Co, 1924), p.260

147 Richardson, *Fifty Years with Dogs*, p.42

148 B.W. Procter, *English Songs and Other Small Poems by Barry Cornwall* (London, 1832), pp.25–6

149 'Death Of "Caesar"', *The Times*, Issue 40502, 20 April 1914, p.10

150 Ibid.

151 Bonhams Auctions, Lot 122, 14 August 2009, 'A unique "Caesar" car mascot formerly the property of His Majesty King Edward VII, circa 1905' www.bonhams.com/auctions/17327/lot/122/ (accessed 07/02/2016)

152 G. Mast, 'Kracauer's Two Tendencies and the Early History of Film Narrative' in *Critical Inquiry* (Chicago: University of Chicago Press, Vol. 6, No.3); C.M. Hepworth, *Came the Dawn: Memories of a Film Pioneer* (Phoenix House Limited, 1951)

153 Hepworth, *Came the Dawn*, p.67

154 Ibid., p.122

155 A. Birkin, *J.M. Barrie and the Lost Boys*, (London: Constable and Company, 1979), p.30

156 Ibid, p.98

157 W.A. Darlington, *J.M. Barrie* (London: Blackie & Sons Limited, 1938), p.100

158 E.H. Richardson, *British Dogs their Training and Psychology* (London: Skeffington & Son Ltd), p.97

159 Richardson, *Forty Years with Dogs*, p.235

160 H.S. Lloyd 'The Dog in War' in *The Book of the Dog*, p.180

161 'The Blue Cross and Dogs' from the Blue Cross archive, February 2013. Reproduced by kind permission of The Blue Cross

162 E.S. 'Scottie' in *Blue Cross Book of Poems* (London: Jarrolds Publishers Limited, 1917), p.50

163

Blue Cross Annual Reports 1917. Reproduced by kind permission of The Blue Cross

164 R. Johns (ed.) *Nurse Cavell: Dog Lover* (London: Methuen & Co. Ltd., 1934), p.10

165 Ibid., p.14

166 'The Sinking of the Ship' in *The Times*, Monday, 4 January 1915, p.9

167 W.J.B., 'A Diary of an Officer with the 4th Northumberland Fusiliers in France and Flanders'. (By kind permission of the Trustees of the Fusiliers Museum of Northumberland)

168 British Library: The Campaign for Suffrage, www.bl.uk/learning/histcitizen/21cc/struggle/suffrage/background/suffragettesbackground.html (accessed 10/02/2016)

169 'The Women at Work' in *Mid-Sussex Times*, 1 September 1914, p.8

170 E. Blyton, *Five on a Hike Together* (London: Hodder & Stoughton Limited, 1955 (1951)), p.9

171 Ibid., p.10

172 Ibid., pp.28–9

173 'The Blue Cross and Dogs' from the Blue Cross archive, February 2013. Reproduced by kind permission of The Blue Cross

Sniffy

174 Ibid.
175 PDSA Dickin Medal for Gallantry, www.pdsa.org.uk/what-we-do/animal-honours/the-dickin-medal (accessed 07/02/2016)
176 P. Hawthorne, *The Animal Victoria Cross: The Dickin Medal* (Barnsley: Pen & Sword Military, 2014 (2012)), p.25
177 D. Long, *The Animals' VC for Gallantry or Devotion* (London: Preface, 2012), pp.194–5
178 PDSA Dickin Medal for Gallantry, www.pdsa.org.uk/what-we-do/animal-honours/the-dickin-medal (accessed 07/02/2016)
179 'Able Seaman Just Nuisance, R.N.', Simon's Town Tourist Information www.simonstown.com/tourism/nuisance/nuisance.htm (accessed 01/02/2016)
180 Ibid.
181 PDSA Dickin Medal for Gallantry, www.pdsa.org.uk/what-we-do/animal-honours/the-dickin-medal (accessed 07/02/2016)
182 Long, *The Animals' VC for Gallantry or Devotion*, p.67
183 PDSA Dickin Medal for Gallantry, www.pdsa.org.uk/what-we-do/animal-honours/the-dickin-medal (accessed 07/02/2016)
184 Hawthorne, *The Animal Victoria Cross*, p.93
185 Ibid., p.95
186 PDSA Dickin Medal for Gallantry, www.pdsa.org.uk/what-we-do/animal-honours/the-dickin-medal (accessed 07/02/2016)
187 PDSA Dickin Medal for Gallantry, www.pdsa.org.uk/what-we-do/animal-honours/the-dickin-medal (accessed 07/02/2016)
188 Lloyd, *The Book of the Dog*, p.187
189 Long, *The Animals' VC for Gallantry or Devotion*, p.3
190 Ibid., pp.3–5
191 Ibid., p.7
192 Ibid., p.3
193 Hawthorne, *The Animal Victoria Cross*, pp.116–7
194 Ibid., p.117
195 K. Williams, *Young Elizabeth: The Making of our Queen* (London: Weidenfeld & Nicolson, 2012), p.68
196 B. Hoey, *Life with the Queen* (Gloucestershire: Sutton Publishing, 2006), p.113
197 Ibid.
198 *The Kennel Club's Illustrated Breed Standards: The Official Guide to Registered Breeds* (London: Ebury Press, 1998) p.337
199 The Magic Roundabout, BFI Screen Online www.screenonline.org.uk/tv/id/591175/ (accessed 26/01/2016)
200 Ibid.
201 *The Kennel Club's Illustrated Breed Standards*, p.254
202 'The Dog License Fund' from the Blue Cross archives, February 2013. Reproduced by kind permission of The Blue Cross
203 Ibid.
204 Ibid.
205 M. O'Neill et al, 'West Sussex Literary Musical & Artistic Links', (West Sussex County Council, 1993), pp.22–3
206 Animals in War Memorial: Home www.animalsinwar.org.uk/index.cfm?asset_id = 1373 (accessed 07/02/2016)
207 Animals in War Memorial: The Monument www.animalsinwar.org.uk/index.cfm?asset_id = 1374 (accessed 07/02/2016)
208 A. Croxton Smith, 'The Dog in History' in *The Book of the Dog*, p.47
209 Petplan Pet Census 2011, p.3, downloaded from www.petplan.co.uk/petcensus/ (accessed 03/09/2015)
210 Ancestry.com blog 'Pet Census – Britain's historic love affair with animals revealed' http://blogs.ancestry.com/uk/2014/01/30/pet-census-britains-historic-love-affair-with-animals-revealed/ (accessed 3/9/2015)
211 1911 Census, Class: RG14; Piece: 17982; Schedule Number: 278

Pippa

212 1911 Census, Class: RG14; Piece: 2457
213 Dalziel, *British Dogs*, p.156
214 Ibid., p.375
215 J.H. Walsh, *Dogs of the British Islands: A Series of Articles on The Points of their Various Breeds* (London: Horace Cox, 1882), p.122
216 P. Corballis, *Pub Signs* (Luton: Lennard Publishing, 1988), p.99
217 S. Pepys, *The Diary of Samuel Pepys*, edited by R.C. Lathan and W. Matthews, Volume 1 – 1600, (London: G. Bell and Sons Ltd, 1971 (1970)), entry for 23 August 1660, p.230
218 J. Simpson, *Green Men & White Swans: The Folklore of British Pub Names* (London: Arrow Books, 2011 (2010)), pp.15–8
219 Correspondence with Jim Payne regarding the former Black Dog pub in Yapton, West Sussex (11/02/2016)
220 J. Larwood and J. Camden Hotten, *English Inn Signs: A Revised and Modernised version of The History of Signborads* (Exeter: Blaketon Hall Limited, 1985 (1951)), pp.127–8
221 Ibid., p.127
222 Ibid., p.128
223 L. Dunkling and G. Wright, *Pub Names of Britain: The Stories Behind over 10,000 Names* (London: JM Dent, 1993), pp.74–5
224 'Most common names of open pubs listed on Pubs Galore' www.pubsgalore.co.uk/stats/pubs/pub-names/ (accessed 11/02/2016)
225 *The Kennel Club's Illustrated Breed Standards*, p.279
226 H. Soteriou, 'Inside Hyde Park's Secret Pet Cemetery', www.telegraph.co.uk/travel/news/Inside-Hyde-Parks-secret-pet-cemetery/ (accessed 28/01/2016)
227 'The Royal Kennels' on The Official Website of the British Monarchy, www.royal.gov.uk/TheRoyalHousehold/RoyalAnimals/Workinganimals/TheRoyalKennels.aspx (accessed 02/02/2016)
228 The Kennel Club: Press Release October 2015, www.thekennelclub.org.uk/press-releases/2015/october/meet-britain%E2%80%99s-surprising-new-pedigree-dog-breed-%E2%80%93-the-jack-russell-terrier/ (accessed 03/02/2016)
229 The Artist Awards, The Internet Movie Database www.imdb.com/title/tt1655442/awards?ref_=tt_awd (accessed 05/02/2016)
230 Information from 'St John the Baptist and St Andrew's Church Kemberton: A Guide for Visitors'
231 *The Kennel Club's Illustrated Breed Standards*, p.306
232 Walsh, *Dogs of the British Islands*, p.198
233 Vulnerable Native Breeds, www.thekennelclub.org.uk/getting-a-dog-or-puppy/finding-the-right-dog/vulnerable-native-breeds/ (accessed 07/02/2016)
234 Stall, *100 Dogs Who Changed Civilization: History's Most Influential Canines*, pp.30–1
235 Jesse, *Researches into the History of the British Dog, from Ancient Laws, Charters and Historical Records*, p.132
236 Ibid., pp.132–3
237 *The Times*, 28 March 1992
238 *Observer*, 23 April 2006, p.11
239 'An Emotional Reunion' in *Newshound*, Summer 2011
240 'Dudie's Diary' in *Newshound*, Summer 2011
241 All the information in this section comes from The Kennel Club: Vulnerable Native Breeds, www.thekennelclub.org.uk/getting-a-dog-or-puppy/finding-the-right-dog/vulnerable-native-breeds/ (accessed 07/02/2016)
242 Richardson, *Fifty Years*, p.173.